Stuart Symington

PORTRAIT OF A MAN
WITH A MISSION

By

PAUL I. WELLMAN

SELIN
+

B
Sy 6w

DOUBLEDAY & COMPANY, INC.
GARDEN CITY, NEW YORK
1960

Library of Congress Catalog Card Number 60-6174
Copyright © 1960 by Paul I. Wellman
All Rights Reserved
Printed in the United States of America
First Edition

TO EVELYN WADSWORTH SYMINGTON
A TRULY GREAT LADY

CONTENTS

I. THE "IMPOSSIBLE" THAT WAS POSSIBLE   11

II. A MAN SHOWS HIS METTLE   27

III. A PRODIGY IN POLITICS   41

IV. THE BEGINNINGS OF STUART SYMINGTON   53

V. THE FORMATIVE YEARS   69

VI. THE GIRL OF THE GENESEE VALLEY   81

VII. THE EMERGENCY AT EMERSON   95

VIII. "A LOAD OF COAL"   111

IX. THE WAY OF A PUBLIC SERVANT   121

X. THE PRESIDENT'S TROUBLE SHOOTER   133

XI. A FRESHMAN SENATOR   151

XII. THE MCCARTHY ORDEAL   167

XIII. A "FAVORITE SON" AND THE DEFENSE ISSUE   185

XIV. THE WARNING   195

XV. TO THE PEOPLE FOR THEIR VERDICT   209

XVI. A BID FOR WORLD DISARMAMENT   219

XVII. STRENGTH: THE ROAD TO PEACE   233

XVIII. LEVELHEADED LIBERAL   245

XIX. "ONE ISSUE?" OR "BIGGEST ISSUE?"   261

XX. STUART SYMINGTON TODAY   273

STUART SYMINGTON

I

THE "IMPOSSIBLE"
THAT WAS POSSIBLE

1

They said it couldn't be done.

Was it actually true that an amateur, without political backing or experience, had the temerity to step into Missouri's arena and challenge in an election a proved vote-getter, an "old pro" with the state's most powerful political leaders behind him?

On the face of it, the thing seemed ridiculous to the seasoned old politicians. Almost laughable, indeed, if you didn't feel sorry for the poor fellow, who obviously didn't know where he was going, or what he should do, or how impossible was the goal he had set for himself.

Yet there he was, Stuart Symington, announcing his candidacy for the United States Senate in the primaries of 1952, against one of Missouri's most experienced campaigners, J. E. (Buck) Taylor, state attorney general, who had twice won state-wide contests and had been groomed for the place for two years. And to make it even more impossible, there were two other candidates, John A. Johnson, a state senator, commander of the Veterans of Foreign Wars, and president of the Young Democrats, and Roger Slaughter, a former Congressman, both of whom would cut into the votes of Taylor's rival, rather than into those of Taylor himself.

Missouri is a state that takes its politics seriously and plays the game for everything that is in it. Over the years it has developed, particularly in the big population centers, some of the most deadly vote-getting machines in the history of the Nation. And even in the rural districts men and women think hard and size up a candidate long before they cast their ballots for him.

The masters of the political game know every way to reach those voters, in city or country. They have worked themselves from the precinct on up, battling and learning, until they are acquainted with every ruse, every trick of in-fighting, virtually every doorbell where a voter resides. When the orders go out, the district bosses see that the ward leaders perform, and the ward leaders see that the precinct captains get to work, and the precinct captains have their own organizations which canvass their areas as closely as if they were combed.

It is almost impossible for a newcomer to beat an organization like that, and Taylor had it behind him. Furthermore, he had his own personal machine—one hundred deputy attorneys general, almost one to every county in the state, and every one of them personally loyal to him and working for him.

Who was this Stuart Symington, anyway?

Few in Missouri knew him, and most of those only in a vague sort of way, by name. And Missouri does not bear the sobriquet of the Show Me State for nothing. Its voters have to be shown.

Small wonder that when the primary campaign of 1952 started the odds were seven to one that Stuart Symington would get nowhere in his effort to gain the nomination for Senator.

But the politicians for once had miscalculated. They did not know Symington at the time, but they were going to get to know him, and find out about him, and so were the people of the state, in a way that was peculiarly and characteristically his own.

2

Stuart Symington, tall, handsome, and courtly, was fifty years old in the spring of 1952, and became fifty-one on June 26 of that year. He was a member of a fine old Southern family which had been impoverished by the Civil War, and he was self-made in every respect. Though he had a Yale education, he had to borrow money and work his way through school. He began life by doing the hardest and dirtiest kind of manual labor. But he had an inner genius that could not be kept down. From working in a shop he graduated to supervisory, then management positions, and then went out on his own to a series of brilliant business successes which made him a relatively wealthy man. At the top of this success, he suddenly gave up money-making to serve his government in an equally brilliant series of successes as the President's trouble shooter in six different appointive jobs, all of them difficult.

It was true that at the time Symington became a candidate for Senator from Missouri he was perhaps better known in Washington than in his home state. But his opponents misjudged him in some very important particulars.

First, he had a reason for seeking the Senate post; a reason that was beyond mere personal ambition, although he has a healthy amount of that, too; a reason that impelled him to forego much more lucrative and pleasant careers to enter a slugging match in the political cockpit of his state. The reason sounds odd in the light of practical politics, because it was idealistic whereas practical politics is not. He had for six and one-half years closely observed the direction the Nation was going, and the trend of world affairs; and he was alarmed by what he saw and wanted to be where he could do something about it.

Second, he was fully aware of the difficulties confronting him and the odds against him; and he went into the battle with his eyes wide open, accepting the gage for what it was, and knowing that only an extraordinary effort on his part would win.

Third, as his great friend Clark Clifford, a topflight Washington attorney says: "Stuart Symington, if he makes a decision after thinking the matter out, goes to the very bitter end for it. He has the most fully developed competitive spirit of any human being I ever met. This is true in minor things like the sports he enjoys, tennis when he was younger, golf now; he is always a tough man to beat, a fair and clean competitor, but tough. It is even more true in the great matters. That competitive spirit is not only for himself, but more particularly and importantly for the cause for which he is fighting."

In January 1952, Symington had completed a difficult and at the same time very important task, the reorganization and rehabilitation of the Reconstruction Finance Corporation, which had fallen pretty low in public confidence. He was considering the next step in his life, and already he had been approached with three opportunities, all of them most tempting.

Two of these were business offers, extended by firms which were at the top in their fields in the Nation, to a man whom business respected for his achievements in business. These offers included large salaries and important stock purchasing options, which would have seemed like the culmination of a dream of lifetime success and wealth to any ordinary man.

The third, curiously, and for a characteristic reason, intrigued him perhaps as much as either of the others. An athlete himself, Symington loves sports. He likes to hunt and fish, was a good enough tennis player to qualify for the Boys' National Championships when he was younger, and plays golf today in the middle 70s. One of his loves is baseball. He is a fan who talks knowledgeably about the game and its players, and likes its American traditions and history, believing it is not only fine for the countless thousands who watch it, but for those who play it, from the great professionals to the tiniest Little Leaguers.

An emissary came to him to inquire if, by any chance, he would consider becoming High Commissioner of Baseball. He more than toyed with the thought, for it would have been fun, and he has a great capacity for enjoying life, and it would have been, in its way, an important task.

But in the end he gave up all thoughts of the lush, wonderful jobs with lots of money or the pleasant, intriguing job with baseball, and chose the toughest, meanest, most difficult course the alternatives offered—to run for the Senate.

Why?

The reasons are once more characteristic of the man.

One of his friends in St. Louis is a famous and revered lawyer, Jacob M. Lashly, a lifelong Democrat, former president of the American Bar Association, and, incidentally, head of the law firm of which Clark Clifford, Symington's close friend, had been a partner, before he became head of his own firm in Washington.

The times ahead seemed dark, and Lashly, a man of monumental integrity and patriotism, with some other farseeing and national-minded Democrats, was concerned that the government should have the best and strongest men who could be induced to take part in it.

When Symington returned home to St. Louis from Washington, this group of men approached him with the suggestion that he run for the Senate. His reply was immediate and unhesitating: "I am not a politician, and I have no political ambitions."

But Lashly was one man who would not accept this verdict.

Symington was deeply concerned about the future of the Nation. He had seen things he did not like in governmental procedures in Washington. He had seen, also, what he considered a short-sighted and dangerous policy of allowing the weakening, in the name of economy, of the defense system of the United States. He had seen the rising power of Communism, and as he has expressed it: "We know that Communism is faithless and aggressive, that its designs are directed to conquest, and that its promises are meaningless." He it was who accurately foretold, before anyone else in high government office, the upsurge of the war-making power of Russia until it surpassed that of America.

Lashly knew Symington's remarkable abilities, and he felt they should be placed at the disposal of the Nation. One day, after listening to Symington's passionate expression of his fears for the country, and his opinions concerning things that should be done, he said:

"Stuart, if you believe that way, you have no right to allow yourself the luxury of going back to making money."

The veteran lawyer knew his man. Put that way, his statement probably was what finally decided Stuart Symington.

Already, however, before that final clinching thought, he

had considered seriously the suggestion that had been made to him of making the Senate race. There is not much question that it had elements that appealed to him, even while he rejected it.

His six and one-half years of government service, first as Surplus Property Administrator, then successively as Assistant Secretary of War for Air, Secretary of the Air Force, Chairman of the National Security Resources Board, and Administrator of the RFC, had given him a tremendous lift. He had sensed the breadth and importance of the Nation's business, and he was not happy over some of the things he had encountered in its management.

He knew the seriousness of the problems confronting his Nation, and he felt, in all modesty, that he had something perhaps unusual in experience and ability to offer. Although he was not wealthy in the modern sense, his business career had left him comfortably independent, his money invested in trusts, so that he did not feel that he might perhaps be jeopardizing his family's interests or future.

Finally, there was the tradition of public service, not only of his own but his wife's family. Evelyn Wadsworth Symington, daughter of the late Senator James A. Wadsworth, is the lovely flower of a long family line which has been outstanding in sometimes dramatic incidents of public service since colonial times in America. Symington's own father had been a judge in Baltimore, Maryland, and his mother was a Harrison of Virginia.

There is no question in the mind of one of his closest associates that the tradition of public service behind him was an actuating influence on the wonderfully sensitive mind of Stuart Symington.

But it required Jacob Lashly's blunt statement, laying on

the line a choice between private gain and public duty, to
bring about his final decision.

3

So the decision was made; but before he issued any formal
statement, Symington closely studied the problems before
him with Lashly, Clifford, and others. The difficulties must
have seemed almost insurmountable to anyone less determined than he was. Some of them were as follows:

First, he had never been in politics, had nothing of the
knowledge of political strategy or technique, did not possess
the training in so-called practical politics which is acquired
by the man who works up through the precinct, ward, and
on higher. His father had been in politics to the extent that
he was appointed to the position of Associate Justice of the
Supreme Bench of Baltimore, which he occupied until his
death in 1926. Other than this, Symington's only connection
with politics had been when he sold peanuts, chewing gum,
and chocolates as a ten-year-old boy at a Democratic convention; and when as a cub reporter on the *Baltimore Sun* he had
written some local political news stories; and of course his
learning to get along as an executive administrator with various Senators, Congressmen, and other public officials during
his service in Washington. This fringe politics was no help
to him now. He had never run for office, or even worked in a
political campaign before.

Second, it was a tradition in Missouri—and Missouri is a
state that is long and strong on traditions—that a man who
ran for high office should be a native-born Missourian, and
it was better if his father was born in Missouri before him,
and it was even better yet if his grandfather was born in

Missouri also—the longer the continuous line of Missourians, the more acceptable the candidate. But Symington was born in Amherst, Massachusetts; lived most of his youth in Maryland from which his family originally hailed; began his business life in New York; and did not come to Missouri until 1938, when he was thirty-seven years old. He had, then, been a Missourian for only fourteen years in 1952, and even that relatively short residence was cut into by his continuous governmental services from 1945 on. By contrast all three of his opponents were from old Missouri families.

Third, there was a historical precedent in Missouri that one Senator should always be from the eastern half of the state, the other from the western half. But already there was a Senator from eastern Missouri, Senator Thomas Carey Hennings, Democrat. And what made it more difficult, Senator Hennings lived in St. Louis, the very city in which Symington resided. On the other hand, Taylor who opposed him in the primaries, and the incumbent, Senator James P. Kem, Republican, both were from the western part of the state.

Fourth, Taylor was an experienced campaigner, whose connections with the most powerful Democratic political machines, and his state-wide system of deputies, had a ready-made vote-getting organization already functioning. Symington's advisors would not be able to match the political experience and connections of that organization.

Fifth, it was inevitable that Symington would be tagged as a "big business" candidate, a member of the country club set, a rich man who knew nothing of the common people's problems, a high-society sprig who, as his opponent actually said later, "did not have a speaking acquaintance with one hundred people in Missouri, outside of St. Louis." All of this was untrue, in the sense that it was designed to mean, but he must find some means to answer it and combat it.

All of this would seem sufficient, but there was still one more handicap that Symington and his friends had not anticipated. President Harry Truman had called him to Washington years before to take a difficult and thankless job, and then had kept him continuously in service as his trouble shooter. More than once the President had expressed his high approval of Symington's ability and achievements, and also his personal friendship.

So Symington went to the White House to ask for support in the forthcoming primary. It would have been an enormous boost to his prospects to have the backing of the man who was not only the most powerful Democrat in Missouri, but in the Nation.

He began his interview with enthusiasm, but as he talked he wondered at what he felt was Truman's lack of answering enthusiasm. When he finished, the President said, after a moment's thought, "I couldn't be sorrier, Stu, but I've already made a commitment to Buck Taylor. It's just too bad. I had no idea you would ever take it into your head to run for the Senate."

As a matter of fact, Harry Truman had made his promise two years before. In 1950, Buck Taylor, an old friend of Truman's, came to him to ask his support in the Senate race. At that time the President counseled against it. But he ended by saying that if Taylor would wait, he would be glad to support him in 1952, against the Republican incumbent, Senator Kem, who had consistently opposed every administration policy.

Symington knew that Harry Truman was not the man to go back on his word, any more than he was himself. So he did not argue the matter. But it was a terrible letdown for him. In that moment he suffered one of his few real periods of discouragement.

4

There is a sequel to the Truman interview. The President was in an unhappy position and he knew it. Stuart Symington had done a magnificent job for him, wherever he had been put, and was a member of his official family. Truman was very high on Symington's ability and integrity, and was personally fond of him. Furthermore, he owed him, to a degree, a debt of gratitude.

But he had made a commitment, and he kept it. The manner in which he kept it, however, was unique.

Shortly after the campaign fight between Symington and Taylor grew hot, the President flew to Missouri. As he got off the plane, he was met by a crowd of reporters, who asked him which of the two Senatorial candidates he was for.

"I'm for Buck Taylor," said Truman.

"Why?" was the next question.

"Because," said the President, "every time I have run for office Buck Taylor has been for me, and now that he is running for office, I'm for Buck Taylor."

He had declared his official position, and announced that he would vote for Taylor. But he put it in such a way that it in no way reflected any condemnation of Symington.

Parenthetically, although Harry Truman officially was for Taylor, Bess Truman, good-humoredly, was not. And neither was their daughter Margaret. It is said that there was some family joking over the matter, due to the circumstance that for almost the only time in history the Trumans were divided on an issue, and the President was outvoted by his own household.

Once the primary was out of the way, Truman became one of Symington's strongest supporters.

5

But all this was in the future, and after his interview with the President, Symington returned rather gloomily to St. Louis to ponder the logic of embarking on a fight in which every possible factor seemed to be against him.

That he decided, in the end, to go on with it in spite of all the discouraging circumstances, is one of the best indications of what, in sports parlance, is called "a fighting heart."

On January 15, 1952, he resigned from the RFC, and received from President Truman (perhaps significantly) the Distinguished Service Medal, for "distinguished service to the United States of America in positions of great responsibility."

Thereafter he spent the next six weeks traveling about Missouri, making contacts and talking to local city and county leaders and newspaper editors, and gathering about him a set of aides and advisors.

One interesting interview was with Roy Roberts, head of the *Kansas City Star*, a strongly Republican paper which certainly would not support a Democrat in the election. But Roberts has a strong sense of public responsibility, and after Symington had talked to him for awhile, he said, in something very closely paraphrasing Jacob Lashly's words, "If you feel that way, Mr. Symington, you have no right not to run for the Senate."

One of his more fortunate contacts was made with Stanley Fike, a newspaperman who had been president of the Missouri

Press Association, and who was no mean politician in his own right, having just been elected to the Kansas City school board. He asked Fike to be co-ordinator of his campaign, saying earnestly:

"Stan, the future of the Free World might well be decided in the next few years."

Fike, a sober and conscientious citizen of his country, who had from his editorial chair observed with increasing concern the state of national and world affairs, thought it over and agreed, because he believed Symington was the right man for the office. But he had something of his own to say:

"If the election were held tomorrow, you would be beaten two to one. You say you intend to take it to the people. That will mean a lot of traveling and a lot of work. Are you willing to spend four days a week visiting out over the state?"

Symington said he was. As a matter of fact, as it turned out, he spent not four but seven days a week at it. Fike has countless contacts, especially among the newspaper editors of Missouri, is a good thinker, wonderful at detail, and from the first Symington has relied upon him tremendously.

Jacob Lashly, of St. Louis, organized and became chairman of the "Symington for Senator Citizens Committee" which was an active spearhead in winning "amateur" support in the primary to come and the election following.

There was some little difficulty finding the proper treasurer. For one reason or another, none of the Democrats around Symington were exactly suited for the job. One day he was talking to Sidney Maestre, chairman of the board of the Mercantile Trust Company, of St. Louis, perhaps the leading financial figure in Missouri. Maestre is a Republican, but he was interested in Symington because of mutual friendship.

"How are they coming in their search for a financial chairman?" he asked.

"They haven't found one yet," confessed Symington.

"How would they like a Republican to serve?"

"Why, they'd take a Republican gladly, as long as they knew he was a good man."

"Well, how about me?" asked Maestre.

It was an astounding piece of good luck, because Maestre's standing and integrity, coupled with that of Lashly, gave dignity and solidity to the whole Symington organization.

At the suggestion of Sidney Salomon, Jr., former treasurer of the Democratic National Committee, Symington asked James H. Meredith to be his campaign manager. Meredith, from the "Boot Heel" country of Missouri, was a political protegé of Governor Forrest Smith, serving as attorney for the State Insurance Commission. Through Meredith, Symington got the backing of the retiring Governor, an important influence in down-state Missouri.

Jim Meredith likes to call himself "a big country boy," but he has great ability and shrewdness, and he was one of the few professionals in the Symington organization, with a knowledge of politics from the precinct up.

With such a nucleus, Symington himself labored tremendously. The month and a half of groundwork was amazingly revealing in its results. One political observer, Ed Woods, writing in the *St. Louis Post-Dispatch*, said:

What he [Symington] put together during a few short weeks after he decided to run for the nomination was the type of political machine Rube Goldberg could draw cartoons about. Its components were bankers, labor leaders, battle-scarred ward heelers, country editors, starry-eyed liberals, dyed-in-the-wool reactionaries, Republicans, Democrats, Dixiecrats, dedicated

"Do-gooders," fugitives from Jim Pendergast's power grab, Sheriff Thomas F. Callanan [of St. Louis] and those who were out to slit Callanan's throat.

That impressive crazy quilt of support was a tribute to one thing: Stuart Symington's matchless ability to win the friendship and fealty of the people with whom he comes into contact. When you talk with him, and watch him for awhile, you somehow come to believe in him as you have believed in few other men in your lifetime.

II

A MAN SHOWS HIS METTLE

1

The time had come to begin the great adventure, and even with all the loyalty and work he received from his friends and aides, it was apparent from the very beginning that the burden of the campaign would fall on Stuart Symington himself, and on nobody else.

With great clarity he saw what he must do, and he laid out his own strategy. For a man who was relatively unknown to the people of a state, there was only one way to win in an election which was state-wide and therefore furnished far greater problems than an election more limited, as in a Congressional or city election. Such a man simply must introduce himself to the people of the state. And in so doing he must somehow get across to them his policies and beliefs, and convince them of his sincerity and integrity, and also his ability to serve them.

That was what he set out to do and it was a herculean task he undertook. Before it was finished it meant an unprecedented 27,000 miles of travel by automobile, and uncounted thousands more by plane and train. It meant visiting ninety of Missouri's one hundred and fourteen counties; going into every possible town and city, big or little; meeting, chatting with, and making friends of the people.

That he accomplished it was only possible because of his tremendous drive.

"He's like a rocket engine," says Clark Clifford. "That great competitive spirit of his has won for him many times when he might have lost. 'I don't want to be a good loser, I want to be a good winner,' is one of his smiling sayings. And it's true. He wants anything with which he identifies himself to win—his business in the old days, his department in government later, his party, his state, most particularly his nation."

The first step was a formal announcement. At Paris, Missouri, in the area of counties known as "Little Dixie" along the Missouri River, the late Jack Blanton was editor of the newspaper. Blanton was, in his way, a rather celebrated veteran journalist. He was once singled out by a national magazine as the type-perfect country editor. He had dry humor, deep understanding of the people of his community and state, and a clear view of events and trends. Jack Blanton wrote a note:

Dear Symington: Some of us up here are interested in you running for the Senate. Sincerely, Jack Blanton.

That was all, characteristically of Blanton. But it had an unexpected effect. It determined Symington on opening his campaign in Paris.

On March 21, Stuart and Mrs. Symington and a few others, including Stan Fike, traveled to Paris. Recalling that day, Fike says, quizzically:

"For his first speech in any political campaign, Symington had a packed house—but the house held only thirty-five people. He made his speech, and I've heard better, but none more earnest. It wasn't long, but it was convincing. He said simply that he had decided to run because he believed that he could be of further service to the people of Missouri in such fields as taxation, efficient rearmament, and clean government."

Afterward, Symington went up and down the streets of Paris, calling on all the people he could, in his warm pleasant way, introducing himself and asking for their support. Meantime Evelyn Symington, playing in perfect harmony with her husband, visited with the women of the town, and charmed them completely. When the Symington party left, Paris, Missouri, was a Symington political stronghold.

From that day on there was to be no rest.

The entire Symington family took part very earnestly. The elder son, Stuart, who is called Tim, aided Jim Meredith in the campaign headquarters office. The second son, Jim, then a law student, is a talented singer and entertainer, who at one time had his own television and night club show. He was the forerunner of the electioneering party. With a sound truck he would arrive in a town about twenty minutes before his father and mother. During that time he would entertain the crowd that gathered with songs, guitar playing, and an amusing patter of stories and jokes.

On the arrival of the main party, Jim would move on to the next point in the itinerary, to gather another crowd. Stuart Symington would take over, make a brief talk—never long—which was angled toward one or two issues of especial interest in that community, and afterward go up and down the street, introducing himself, shaking hands, visiting, making friends.

His manner of approach was unaffectedly simple. "My

name is Stuart Symington," he would say. "I'm running for the Senate, and I hope you will vote for me."

The smile that went with this was well-nigh irresistible. And so was the sincerity behind it.

Meantime Mrs. Symington was doing an equally beautiful job of making friends. She went to church meetings, or schools, or homes, or stores, and wherever she went she won the hearts of the women, and also the men, with whom she talked. It would be hard to overstate her importance in this campaign.

Symington, in one respect, had a rather delicate, feather-edge task to perform in his first meeting with the people of Missouri. It is best described by John H. Zentay, then a student at Harvard, who analyzed the astonishing Symington campaign as a subject for a thesis looking to a degree. Wrote Zentay:

> Though a novice at campaigning, Symington knew his Missouri politics. "Most important thing in a campaign," he said, "is to be natural; country people can spot a phony as well as city folks. So one important thing is don't talk down to anybody and don't dress down."
>
> So he went out on an intensive and extensive tour through the state, showing the people that he was "just plain Stu" Symington, shortened from W. Stuart Symington III, and also the dapper Yale graduate in Brooks Brothers button-downs who had "held all those high jobs in Washington." He wanted the people of Missouri to know that he was "one of them," but that he was also "one of them" who knew his way around Washington and could be counted on to do a competent job. This, of course, is the double impression which all candidates for office seek to give the voters; it is a difficult one to create and depends on the candidate's personality more than on his speech writers. Judging from the results, Symington was eminently successful.

He was what Herbert Trask termed "a business executive with a folksy touch."

Actually, however, there was not much opportunity for Symington to dress in a "dapper" fashion, even if he had wished to do so. Missouri, in the summer, is inclined to be torrid, with a blistering sun blazing down from a superheated sky, and enough humidity to make a penguin in an icebox swelter. Little wanton breezes that spring up soon perish miserably of heat prostration.

With the thermometer throbbing at the one hundred degree mark or above, Missourians humorously are wont to ask new arrivals in their town if the "warm spell" extends to whence these persons have come. And the reply frequently is, "It ain't what you'd call chilly. The present thaw appears to be general all over the country."

"Sometimes it was so hot," Mrs. Symington said later, with a reminiscent smile, "that there wouldn't be a soul on Main Street but us—and maybe a stray cat."

Symington did a large part of his campaigning in shirt sleeves, mopping his face from time to time with a handkerchief, and the fact that he could smile and appear cheerful, even happy, in the midst of a heat wave warmed the hearts of Missourians to him. He was one of them, assuredly, since he came in all this hot weather to say, "Howdy."

It did not bother Symington. Heat or no he kept up his pace, and as one person said, "He wore down everyone around him."

The truth of the matter is that he was enjoying himself hugely. He is companionable, and he likes people, and it was fun to go around and meet new folks, and make friends, and see where they lived, and find out what they wanted in a man they might send to the Senate. That is one of his outstanding characteristics. No one can call Stuart Symington "home-spun." On the other hand he is "folksy," and it is as much a part of him as the long legs on which he strides around. People take to him because he takes to them. It's mutual and it works well both ways.

A typical day during the campaign would begin about eight o'clock in the morning, with a breakfast to which local Democratic leaders, or editors of the papers in the district, were invited. Symington invariably made a point of conferring with the newspaper people as soon as he arrived in a community, and at this breakfast each day his guests would brief him on the way people felt about various matters, and what to expect from them.

Thereafter followed the routine of the sound truck, Jim Symington's entertainment before his father's arrival, then the speech, and the mingling with the crowd, while the truck moved on to another locality. The day continued as long as people wanted to see and hear the candidate and his family, and his energy and activity were almost incredible. In one single day, for example, he spoke in twenty-two towns in one county. At another time he covered twenty-three counties in ten days.

Missouri and Missourians are famous for hospitality, and it would be hard to total the number of ham breakfasts, basket luncheons, and fried chicken and covered-dish suppers he attended, in shirt sleeves like as not. And though he eats sparingly, he enjoys good food, and in particular he enjoys the relaxed atmosphere that surrounds such affairs. He talked to men and women, and he listened more than he talked, and when he moved on they did not forget him.

But at night Symington always stayed at a hotel in town,

gracefully excusing himself from invitations to the homes of local politicians or eminent citizens, "so that he might talk with a few more people in the lobby before going to bed."

It was an old-fashioned kind of campaign, almost a horse and buggy campaign, "one that seemed to many people a relic of the Lincoln-Douglas debate days," as Zentay says. It was so old, in fact, that it was new, and Missouri loved it. That Symington, most modern and up-to-date of men, should have adopted it made it more remarkable, and it was an evidence of his exact appraisal of his problem and the tactics to overcome it. The effectiveness of those tactics was sensational, so much so that it became alarmingly evident to his opposition before many weeks that the strongest measures must be taken to counteract them.

2

Another thing evidenced itself, somewhat belatedly, to the opposition camp. Stuart Symington had some unsuspected strengths. In his business career he had drawn national attention to his levelheaded and fair manner of treating labor, and labor now reciprocated with a gratitude that made itself manifest in strong political support. He had also, by his attitude and acts, proved to the Negroes that he was their friend, and he had the colored vote rather solidly behind him. Meantime, in St. Louis, the Citizens for Symington had organized a "chain telephone" drive which was garnering plenty of votes.

Buck Taylor, at the beginning, had been inclined to be scornful of his amateur adversary. He had, in fact, been quoted as saying before Symington's formal announcement, "I wish that carpetbagger would run. I'd show him a thing or two."

It was a mistake, because it nettled Symington, and when

he is nettled he becomes more dangerous. He resented the carpetbagger appellation, and he set out to show Taylor that he wasn't a carpetbagger, and that he could teach a few lessons himself.

A seven-to-one favorite at the start of the campaign, Taylor expected a rather easy race of it, in which he would coast to victory. But now, with the new facts, which must have been appalling, confronting him, he began to strike out somewhat desperately.

Throughout that campaign Symington never once went into personalities, or even mentioned the name of his opponent. But some of Taylor's supporters at this point began a series of personal attacks on Symington, his record, even his private life.

As an illustration of the curious low level of this attack, one story was circulated, although not formally published, that Symington had been convicted of stealing a car.

Actually he had gone on a brief joy ride with some other boys in a neighbor's car when he was sixteen years old. He did not take the car nor did he drive it. The youth who was driving succeeded in wrecking the car, and Symington, who had only gone along for the ride, came out of it worse than anybody, receiving a badly broken left arm.

A boyish prank is exactly what the episode amounted to, but it was magnified into a bona fide car theft by the opposition's whispering campaign.

There is no question but that the story disturbed Symington, who was new to politics, and particularly gutter politics, and was sensitive to a slur on his good name. One of his veteran advisors laughed about it and said, "Forget it, Stu. That story will only make you votes. There isn't a man living today who was once a real boy, who didn't get into some such sort of a scrape in his youth. They'll chuckle over it and like you the better for it."

But Symington, who has a high sense of honor, honesty, and truth, winced whenever the malicious tale came to his ears from a new source. He was thin-skinned in those days, and it made him unhappy, particularly since he did not know how to answer it.

Then, one day, almost out of the blue, came a letter from the man who owned the car in which the boys took the joy ride. He was still living, and his name was Harry Dorsey Watts, of East Hampton, New York. His letter read as follows:

Dear Stuart:

I was disturbed recently to hear that a boyish prank which occurred years ago had become a distorted political issue. For the record, let me personally set the facts straight:

In 1918, the sons of some neighbors took my car—which was parked unlocked in front of the house—and went for a ride without my permission. You were one of those boys.

The boy who drove, who, as I remember, was not you, missed a turn, went into a ditch, and wrecked the car.

Your father, one of my very closest friends, immediately got together with the parents of the other boys and paid me in full for the damage.

It never occurred to me that anything more would come of it, but the accident came up in court and all of you, who had been fined $25, were released in custody of your parents.

At the time, the incident was only a prank, and it is absurd to think that it could be considered anything else thirty-four years later.

With very best wishes,

HARRY DORSEY WATTS.

The letter, from the person most concerned in the episode, greatly relieved Symington's mind, since it completely re-

futed the implications of the whispering campaign. Thereafter, whenever the story arose, the person who had heard it
was sent a photostatic copy of the letter. It created a lot of
chuckles, and in the end reacted strongly in Symington's
favor.

Another, even nastier, but less worrisome story—for by now
the candidate had developed an ability to shrug off calumnies
—was the distribution of a doctored newspaper item, based
on a coincidence in names. According to the article, Lady
Sylvia Ashley, once the wife of Douglas Fairbanks and later
of Clark Gable, had been in an automobile accident in the
Bahama Islands. The car turned over, and "out rolled Stuart
Symington." Stuart Symington was described as "tall, dark,
and 29 years old."

That description, which at once would have prevented any
confusion since the Missourian at the time was fifty-one
years old and blond, was edited out by someone and a line
added, "now married to Evelyn Wadsworth." This libelous
story was circulated in handbills and even dropped from an
airplane in some districts.

Newspapers later saw to it that the correct account was
published. It developed that the Stuart Symington of the
Bahama accident was one Captain Stuart Symington, Royal
Air Force, aide to the Governor of the Bahamas. The name
is Scottish, which accounts for its duplication in Britain and
in America.

Again this distortion reacted in Symington's favor. His
attorneys told him he could collect damages in court for the
willful libel, but he laughed about it, and told one of his
favorite stories to illustrate his opinion of it.

"It's just 180 degrees wrong," he said. "It reminds me of
a man who came home and told his wife, 'Honey, I've had a

big day—I sold a thousand shares of General Motors stock and made a hundred thousand dollars.'

"The wife said, 'George, you're always exaggerating. Now tell me the truth.'

"The man thought a minute and then said, 'Well, it wasn't exactly that way, Honey. It wasn't a thousand shares, it was a hundred. It wasn't General Motors, it was I. B. M. It wasn't a hundred thousand dollars, it was ten thousand. And I didn't make it, I *lost* it.' "

One episode occurred during the campaign which gave Symington a momentary scare, and it is worth recounting because it shows the family ability to react directly, quickly, and properly in an emergency.

Coming into Tarkio, Missouri, where his son Jim as usual had preceded him, Symington found the sound truck and a crowd about it, but no Jim.

When he asked where his son was, a man replied, "Someone's been shot."

There was a natural moment of acute concern on the father's part. Then came the explanations.

What happened was, while Jim was entertaining the crowd, a car came careening around a corner and smashed into the curb. Jim went over to find out what the trouble was, and saw a young man and a young woman in the car, which now was stationary.

"He just shot me," gasped the girl.

Hardly able to believe his ears, Jim asked the young man if it was true.

"Yes, it's true," said the man, "and I'm going to shoot you, too."

With that he drew a revolver.

Jim Symington is an athlete. He was a Marine during the

war, and had been a boxer in college. He acted instantly. Leaping on the apparently crazed man, he seized his wrist and a moment later the two of them were rolling over in the street, until Jim wrested the gun away from the other.

Police officers arrived and both young men were taken to the station for inquiry. Meantime investigation showed that the girl had indeed been shot, although as it turned out, the wound was not fatal. Questioning developed these facts: The girl and the young man were married and had quarreled. The husband shot his wife, and perhaps Jim Symington's intervention was all that saved her life.

Jim soon appeared, grinning, and got a cheer from the crowd. The girl was cared for at a hospital. The husband was taken to jail.

"That day Jim got more publicity than I did," says Symington.

3

So the campaign, which had grown steadily more bitter toward the end because of the personalities injected into it by Symington's opposition, drew to a close.

Primary Day was August 5, 1952, and there was a record vote in Missouri.

When the returns were all in, the people of Missouri had overwhelmingly demonstrated that the amateur in politics had shown his professional adversary some very sharp lessons in tactics, and that the personal attacks by his opponent's overzealous supporters had results opposite from those planned.

Symington defeated Taylor by a thumping 368,595 to 180,849, getting a 100,000 majority from St. Louis alone.

There was rejoicing in the Symington headquarters over

the surprising two-to-one victory; but Symington did not particularly take part in it.

He expressed his gratitude to his friends and workers, and to the people who had voted for him, but he knew that he had only crossed the first hurdle. The real contest was yet to come, with a tougher, stronger, meaner opponent.

Senator James P. Kem, the Republican incumbent, with no opposition in the primary, had his party's nod to run for re-election. He was fresh to the fray, and it was apparent already to those close to the political picture that the Republicans were sure to win a sweeping national victory in the fall.

General Dwight D. Eisenhower, a war hero, had been nominated on a platform at once affirmative and aggressive, and evasive and vague, to run for President on the Republican ticket. Governor Adlai Stevenson, the Democratic candidate, was a newcomer to the national picture, and had certain definite handicaps.

Senator Kem, a Kansas City politician, would have Eisenhower's endorsement without question, and if, as seemed probable as early as August, the Republican candidate swept the country in the fall, Kem could "ride in on Eisenhower's coat tails."

Stuart Symington, far from relaxing after his strenuous primary campaign, must get ready for an even grimmer fight for election. He tightened his belt and prepared to enter at once into the coming and crucial battle.

III

A PRODIGY IN POLITICS

1

Senator James P. Kem was one of the leading members of
the so-called Class of '46—that group of conservative Senators who were elected immediately after the close of World
War II. But if his fellow members of that "class" were conservative, Kem himself was so far ahead of them—or behind
them—that he could only be called reactionary.

He was a highly successful corporation lawyer, so thoroughly
identified with the oil business, indeed, that his opponents
tacked the title of James (Petroleum) Kem on him. He had
been chairman of the Jackson County (Kansas City) Republican committee, and knew every politician of any influence
in the state. In his first race for the Senate he was elected
over the incumbent, Frank P. Briggs, by a powerful majority.

In his six years in the Senate, Kem had been industrious in
creating a political machine and building fences in Missouri.
It is probable that when the primary campaign opened and
he supposed like almost everyone else that Buck Taylor would
be his opponent, he looked forward to another rather easy
race, such as he enjoyed in his first candidacy, with the Eisenhower popularity to add to his own carefully tongue-and-

grooved, dovetailed-and-mortised organization, well-cemented with expectations of national patronage.

But by the time of the August primary he was rudely awakened to the realization that he was facing no ordinary opponent, and that he would be extended to the fullest if he expected to win.

Kem knew also that he had a vulnerable record. He was considered the most isolationist member of the Senate, so much so that he was called the Great Aginer, since he voted "agin" every measure that had international implications of any kind. Even members of his own party—at least many of them—felt that he went against them in his extreme rejection of the bipartisan foreign policy.

But Kem was shrewd, and Kem was fast on his feet. He sized up his opponent very quickly, and the conclusions he thus reached caused him to decide that it might be fatal for him to run on his record—especially with Eisenhower advocating a much more enlightened foreign policy than any Senator Kem had favored.

Therefore, the Senator decided to go on the offensive at once, "to hit at Symington with charges against his private and public record before the Democrat could get his high-level campaign rolling." He also made up his mind to emulate Symington's astonishingly successful campaign tactics of going out to meet the people, and in the ensuing months he did make several tours of the state, speaking from sound trucks and the steps of county court houses.

Perhaps in those days Senator Kem began to regret that there was one issue on which he had never voted "no" in the Senate. Repeatedly Stuart Symington had come up for confirmation as he moved from one to another of the trouble-shooting assignments given him by the President. Six times, all told, his name was before the Senate, and six times there was not one single dissenting vote as the Senate unanimously approved his appointment—which was in itself the highest kind of an endorsement of the caliber of work he had been doing.

How poor James P. Kem must have writhed inwardly as he thought of the opportunities he might have had to throw some shadow on his adversary, if by his one vote only. But it was too late now. The record showed he had voted for Symington again and again, and now he was asking the people to vote against the man he had voted for.

Nobody, however, could say that Kem was lacking in cunning or resourcefulness. Or that he did not know the tricks of dirty in-fighting, including all the low blows. With the greatest care he avoided saying anything about his own record, except to mention that he had been "solely interested in the people's welfare." Instead, he began to reiterate the kind of things Buck Taylor's machine backers had uttered during the primary campaign.

One of his gambits was to level his oratory at Symington's relatively short residence in Missouri, and sneer at his social standing, in an appeal aimed at the anti-snobbery and provincialism which he believed, quite wrongly, actuated most of his voters.

Referring to his opponent, Kem called him "the idol of New York cafe society who knows his way around the swank drawing rooms of Park Avenue, New York . . . a Broadway playboy . . . playmate of British royalty . . . the barefoot boy from Baltimore [a steal from Harold Ickes' description of Wendell Willkie] . . . a Wall Street farmer, who never milked anything but a corporation . . . our newly arrived friend from the East . . ." and other terms meant to be galling.

Continually he spoke of his adversary as "W. Stuart Symington III," adding, "He fails to mention that he is related by blood and marriage to some of the richest families in America, and that he was educated in exclusive schools and Yale University."

To this the St. Louis Post-Dispatch somewhat acidly commented, "The speaker [Kem] did not disclose that he is a wealthy corporation attorney and a graduate of Harvard University law school."

As for Symington, he merely smiled. To the charge that he was not a native, he replied, "I am a Missourian by choice, not by accident of birth."

Merely by going his usual way and letting the people see for themselves, he easily dispelled the snobbery charge. Other assertions he dismissed as too trivial for a reply.

In point of fact, this sort of attack on him proved, as in the case of the same tactics in the primary, more of a liability than an asset to Kem, because a majority of the voters considered it underhanded and petty, and disapproved of it accordingly.

But more serious accusations were to follow. Said Kem on one occasion:

"The principal issue in the Missouri Senatorial campaign is special privilege, favoritism, and unjust enrichment in public office. Not only has Mr. Symington personally benefited from some of the uglier aspects of Trumanism but he has made it possible for some of his friends to feather their nests, too. The people have paid heavily for Symington's indiscretions, not only in tax money, but also in delays in our defense efforts brought about by ill-considered, selfishly-inspired projects . . . He is connected with the mess in Washington because he was for six years a pliant and complacent tool of the Truman regime . . . I say to you, Mr. Symington, you have made your bed and you must lie in it."

For the first time this made Symington wince. The charges were all false, but they struck directly at his honesty and integrity, and more than that, they struck at his unselfish devotion to his country, something that is close to his heart.

Yet, in the heat of political debate, such charges are difficult to refute. The eplanations sometimes are long and technical, requiring discussions of financial and statistical matters, which often bore, or go entirely over the heads of audiences. As Zentay wrote, "The charges were easy to make, difficult to answer."

Symington was not then a fluent or easy speaker, and he was perhaps a little nonplused at the beginning. Debate with a practiced orator and courtroom specialist was difficult for a plain-spoken man who all his life had preferred action to words.

During that campaign he and Kem met three times in "old-time, face-to-face, political debates." Each time Kem's glib and orotund style, his ability to flow from one topic to another at will, his self-possessed air of the practiced public speaker, contrasted strongly with Symington's simpler, terser, and more earnest statements.

And yet, a left-handed indication of how well Symington did was contained in the statement of an observer that "most observers felt that Kem came out a little better in the three joint debates."

A *little* better? James P. Kem, with all his experience and eloquence, should have annihilated his less ready opponent. He did not annihilate him, he only did "a little better." And that was a victory for Symington, who was winning, and continuing to win, substantially in other arenas.

Parenthetically, since those days Symington has developed into a very effective speaker. He has gained self-confidence, and states his thoughts well, although he will never be the spread-eagle type of orator. In particular he has become a recognized master in a question-and-answers session, where his phenomenal memory and his manner of marshaling and presenting his facts rarely ever fail to get across his points. There is no stumbling or fumbling for words in Symington's press conferences.

In that 1952 campaign, Senator Kem relied on two massive pieces of artillery to bring him through.

The first was fired on September 20, when General Eisenhower, speaking at Kiel Auditorium in St. Louis, gave Kem a complete endorsement in spite of the latter's record of isolationism, and told the crowd that the Republicans would elect their entire ticket from "top to bottom." He added, "You will elect Howard Elliott as Governor, send Senator Kem to the Senate, and re-elect Claude Bakewell to Congress."

The General proved a bad political forecaster in this instance. All three of the men he named lost in the election that followed.

The second big gun was fired shortly before election day, when it was announced that Senator Joe McCarthy would speak in St. Louis in behalf of Kem. At that time McCarthy was riding high on his drive for power by a reckless application of the "Red" tag to anyone who opposed him.

Said Kem, complacently, believing he had his antagonist trembling at what was to happen, "I think the people of

America owe Senator McCarthy a debt of gratitude for his efforts to drive the Communists out of government."

McCarthy was at that time already perhaps the most feared man in the public eye, with his abusive speeches, and his mudslinging tactics, and in this instance Kem believed he was supplying his advocate the material he could best use. While in private business Symington had dealt with William Sentner, an open Communist, in settling a strike. The fact that Sentner was the head of the union conducting the strike, and that under the Wagner labor law Symington was compelled to deal with him was not mentioned—and made no difference to Kem.

But Symington was unterrified. His comment was: "My opponent has now decided to import that arch-priest of character assassination in the North."

Perhaps he said it a little wearily, but certainly without alarm. For he had learned a great deal already about politics.

His first reactions to vicious onslaughts against his private life and character had been like those of a spirited horse which for the first time feels the savage cut of a whip. Then he gained control of himself, learned to bear the pain, and while he appeared shocked and horrified that such charges should actually be given public utterance in a political campaign, he dismissed them in a general statement that his opponent had resorted to "villifications and untruths" in a desperate effort to win the election.

2

Stewart Alsop, writing in the *St. Louis Post-Dispatch* described the Kem campaign methods as "the Big Doubt Technique." He added that Kem hoped "that the voters [could be] rendered cross-eyed with confusion, so that they would conveniently forget Kem's voting record. Kem has, therefore, attacked Symington on so many fronts that Symington, who has never before had first-hand experience of an election, seems a trifle punch-drunk."

Alsop went on to say, in his article published October 1, 1952:

> One can hardly blame him. It must be an unpleasant experience for a man of hitherto distinguished reputation to find himself simultaneously pictured as a blood-soaked war profiteer, a "golf-playing crony of Communists," and the chosen agent of British international bankers. These three charges against Symington provide typical examples of a political technique which is now widely practiced. The object of this technique is simply to confuse the voters, to raise "the big doubt" in their minds.
>
> Symington sold his stock in the Emerson Electric Company, of which he had been president, when he entered public office. He did so in order to avoid charges of favoring his old company. But the stock had increased in value during Symington's term as president of the company—and so Symington is "a war profiteer."
>
> Symington is a "crony of the Communists" as well as a "blood-soaked capitalist," because a Communist, one William Sentner, once headed the Emerson local union. Symington of course never played golf with Sentner. But, as president of Emerson Electric, he did deal with Sentner on labor matters. Legally, he had no choice. Such fine points, however, do not concern Senator Kem.
>
> Symington is the "stooge of British international bankers" because he once rented a house from a British banker, one Sir William Wiseman. Wiseman is supposed to have selected Symington as his chosen instrument to "punish" Kem for his "pro-American" record. Actually, Symington never laid eyes on this "sinister figure."
>
> This is enough to suggest the nature of Senator Kem's special

political technique. The whole business is amusing enough in some ways, what with Kem's remarkable agility in the attack, and the dazed condition of the novice Symington.

Fortunately—and fortunately especially for Gen. Eisenhower, if he is elected—knowledgeable observers here believe . . . that the voters may be smarter than politicians like Kem think they are.

Mr. Alsop was somewhat in error. Stuart Symington was not punch-drunk, or in a "dazed condition." There is an aphorism in the fight game: "A tramp is no good *when* he gets hurt; a champ is no good *till* he gets hurt."

Symington is a champ. Kem's raw technique only made him more deadly determined to carry that election. Relentlessly he confronted Kem with his record, "the most negative . . . of anyone in the Senate," and listed the long series of measures Kem had voted against, which included not only matters of defense and international relations, but such things close to the hearts of Missouri as agricultural bills and rural electrification.

In one of his better speeches he said that the world situation was "a conflict of ideologies, of values and ultimate goals. We will win only if our faith is genuine and deep." He called for a continual build-up of America's military and economic strength, saying, "I believe firmly in the United Nations and the effort of the Free World to pull together in the cause of peace. But as long as there is the evil of Communism in the world, I believe with Teddy Roosevelt that there is more law in the end of a policeman's night stick than in a judge's gavel."

Of his opponent he said, "He [Kem] is travelling around Missouri talking about the coffins of returning American dead, but who is more responsible for the terrible tragedy of those coffins than a Senator who, before all the world and the

Kremlin, voted against our soldiers and sailors having enough equipment to go into battle?"

Specifically, he asked Kem over and over again, why he "voted in 1949, a year before Korea, to cut defense appropriations by more than 1½ billion dollars and in opposition to taking the fleet out of moth balls? [Why he voted] in 1951, a year *after* Korea's opening guns and while the war was being fought, to slash defense expenditures by 6 billion dollars?"

Such questions Kem found it impossible to answer, but he hoped McCarthy's meat-cleaver speech would put the quietus to his rival.

As it turned out McCarthy's speech, given in St. Louis the Friday before election, backfired rather than helped Kem. The Wisconsin Senator, as Zentay reported, "launched into one of his usual tirades which also included a few remarks about the susceptibility of our college youth to the evil doctrines of Marxism. He was giving the address before a group composed largely of St. Louis University students, and St. Louis University is a Catholic school. The Wisconsin Senator gave the impression he felt many in his audience were in danger of falling under the fellow-traveler influence. The students and faculty members were naturally taken aback by the Senator's apparent lack of faith in their good sense, and coming so close to election time, McCarthy's St. Louis appearance did not help the Kem cause."

McCarthy's personal references to Symington were all old issues such as the dealings with Sentner, which had been thoroughly thrashed out, and were understood. As a matter of fact his speech did the reverse of helping Kem. It hurt him with a good many stalwart Catholics who resented McCarthy's stupid implication that they could be swayed by propaganda from the Kremlin.

So Election Day came, November 4, 1952. It remained only for the votes to be counted.

3

As the results began coming in, there was tension in the Symington headquarters. This was the great and final test, the culmination of months of tremendous effort, the final proof of whether a man with sincere convictions and a mission could win over the machines of cynical professional politicians.

Quite soon, however, the tension began to ease as it became evident that Symington was winning a great personal victory, even though it appeared that Eisenhower would carry the state.

When the full figures became known, the triumph became more astounding.

Symington had defeated his Republican opponent 1,008,521 to 858,170, winning by 55 per cent of the vote and a majority of 150,351—and that in a year of a Republican national sweep. He led Stevenson, the Democratic candidate for President, by 150,000 in round figures, and Eisenhower by 120,000 in round figures.

A miracle had been acomplished, and a new figure appeared on the stage of national politics.

The lesson was apparent to all the politically minded. Stuart Symington is a vote-getter.

Some men are vote-getters, and some just are not. Franklin D. Roosevelt, for example, was a vote-getter. Others have not the same ability.

The quality that makes a vote-getter is something hard to appraise. It is, of course, a matter of personality; and in these days particularly a matter of television personality, since the home set has become the new rostrum of the nation.

It is also a matter of being able to project ideas and the conviction of sincerity, and of impressing the voters that the man before them is one to whom they can well trust the business of government.

It is moreover a matter of making that impression a lasting one. And that was one factor on which Taylor did not count, nor did Senator Kem after him. Once Stuart Symington won a man or a woman to his cause, that man or woman rarely wavered. Later efforts to sway them were futile, no matter how great the pressure and the effort, or what was said or done. The personality of Symington is such that voters feel drawn to him, believe in him, and cherish that faith. And, as he had done many times in his busines career when once men put their faith in him, he justified that faith in his actions thereafter.

Beyond any question, and brilliantly demonstrated in the toughest kind of a test, Stuart Symington belongs to that rare class, seen seldom in the national arena—the men who can win and hold the confidence of the people, the men who get the votes.

Already, when he first stepped upon the floor of the Senate, men wise in politics were beginning to look at him with speculative eyes. He had the look of someone who was going places. The thought that here might be a more than acceptable candidate for the Democratic party in a Presidential election may have suggested itself to some who would be rivals for that high honor, before it did to Symington himself.

IV

THE BEGINNINGS OF
STUART SYMINGTON

1

It would be idle to say that the thought of the Presidency has not entered Stuart Symington's mind. He is too highly intelligent, too honest with himself and others, too well aware of what people think and say of him for that.

Furthermore, he was drafted by the Missouri Democratic convention of 1954, and his name was presented by the Missouri delegation to the National Democratic convention as a favorite son candidate. In the pre-conventon speculation at that time he was widely and favorably commented on as a "dark horse" possibility, and although the convention developed into a three-way race with Stevenson winning the re-nomination, Symington in the balloting received votes from more states, than any other favorite son put forward, in spite of the fact that he made no effort in his own behalf.

The Presidential possibility has to be faced, and increasingly it has been brought to a focus by the press and by individuals in interviewing him.

On April 9, 1959, at a press conference, he expressed his position at the time, when asked if he would refuse a draft movement should a deadlock develop in the coming National convention.

Straightforwardly he replied, "No, I'm in the business of politics. I wouldn't refuse such a movement."

But he added that though he appreciated some of his friends mentioning his name in that connection, he had "no organization and no plans at this time to enter any state primary contests."

Asked at the same time if he favored any particular candidate among those prominently mentioned, he smiled.

"I don't want to make one friend a better friend and lose a lot of other friends," he said. "I will support the Democratic nominee, whoever he is."

Yet the question will not down, and as time passes an increasing number of Democratic leaders are coming to believe not only that Symington would better than anyone else draw together the disparate elements of the party, but that he would be the best campaigner the party could offer, and that he might be the very best man available for the Presidency in either party.

Symington will be fifty-nine years old when the next Presidential campaign takes place, an ideal age for the office. By training, qualities, character, and personality he seems in every respect superbly suited for the highest office in the land.

Physically, Symington is handsome and most impressive. He stands six feet two inches in his socks, and his well-proportioned body, lean without being gaunt, has an athlete's limberness. His weight, about 185 pounds, is the same that it was in his twenties, and he keeps his vigorous body in condition by strict diet and exercise.

Throughout his life he has enjoyed competitive sports and usually excelled in them. As a youth he played baseball, boxed, and was a stellar performer in tennis. Giving up tennis as he grew older, he took up golf; and though he has time to play only once a week, men who go out on the links with him say he could be a tournament player if he took the time to work on his game. At this Symington grins and says golf is a game with him, and never a career.

Aside from golf his sports are hunting and fishing—or anything that gets him out of doors. He is a fine wing shot, and knows the niceties of laying a fly or plug, and setting a hook when a fish strikes. On the wall of his office in the Senate office building is a mounted specimen of a fine bonefish, one of the sportiest game fish in the world, which he caught in Florida. His eye rests on that trophy once in a while with a sportsman's pleased recollection of the day he hooked and landed the silvery racing beauty.

His manner is well-bred, courteous, and pleasant; with women courtly. He speaks with a slight indication of a Southern drawl, natural in a man from the border states and a Southern family. Frequent mention has been made of his charm. One writer in a national magazine reported, "Symington could charm a bird out of a tree." Another man, after talking with him said, "I believe you could sell anybody anything if you really wanted to."

But there is far more to him than charm. Anyone encountering him is at once aware of a striking and compelling personality such as few men possess, with a powerful and forceful mind behind it. Here is a man who could talk on terms of man-to-man equality with Nikita Khrushchev or any other personage in the world, and make his country look good while doing it.

His face is arresting, and his eyes remarkable. A broad, high forehead, well-marked brows, and prominent cheekbones tell not only of his Scottish ancestry, but the tenacity and spirit of the man. A thick thatch of hair, once light brown but now quite gray, is often somewhat rumpled since he has a habit of running his fingers through it when in deep thought or conversation.

His eyes, alert and expressive, and penetrating without being of the gimlet type, are large, deep-set, and dark blue-gray. At the corners are smile wrinkles which often crinkle pleasantly, but between the strong brows are deeply etched lines of concentration. He uses horn-rimmed glasses for reading, but otherwise does not need or wear them.

All told, his features are mobile and reflect his moods and thoughts so appealingly that even his political foes cannot help liking him. His usual expression is pleasant and kindly, but it can become grim as a fighter's visage when his blood is up; and when he is studying a problem or confronted by a moment of stress, it bears a look of intense concentration.

Although in social conversations he likes to jump around from topic to topic, he has the faculty of devoting every bit of his thinking to anything really important in hand. His mind is quick, searching, and of the steel-trap kind that never forgets a fact once it is learned. His pet hate is misinformation. Every fact must be double-checked and he never forgets anyone who gives him a wrong figure or a bad piece of information.

He is no vague theorist—the so-called egg-head type—but his thinking is direct and incisive, though not less profound and broad for all its probing and elastic quality. He reads and studies constantly, and his reading is more serious than anyone knows, except those closest to him.

Busy all day, he reads at night, after going to bed. Books on economics, scientific and technical subjects, reports by experts on current affairs and foreign policy, new developments in this nuclear age are piled on his bedside table. For relaxation he reads history; and is an authority on the Civil War, in which both of his grandfathers fought on the Confederate side, and also on Lincoln, whom he passionately admires. What he considers one of the great portraits of Lincoln hangs in his home.

Summing up, Robert Coughlan perhaps best phrased a feeling one has about him, in an article he wrote for a national magazine:

> Symington is a superior product of nature, a genetic accident of the sort that produces champions in the animal world; he is not merely a thoroughbred but the lucky amalgam of the best in his blood lines.

2

Those blood lines are good, and go back a long way in the history of this country. The first Symington came from Scotland in 1790. He was James Symington, a miller by calling, who set up flour mills in a Delaware village named Brandywine, where thirteen years before, George Washington had fought one of his most famous battles. The village is now swallowed up by the city of Wilmington.

Of his several children, Thomas, great-grandfather of Stuart Symington, was born in Brandywine in 1793. He was, like almost all the Symingtons, very tall—six feet three inches—with blue eyes, and a handsome countenance. Early in his young manhood he gave a demonstration of the family sense of honor. He experienced a business failure, and calling together his creditors, he laid before them so clearly and fully the state of his affairs, that with one accord they gave him a full release of his obligations, on such terms as he could offer. As events proved, they lost nothing by trusting to the integrity of Thomas Symington. A few years later when he had won success, he called another meeting of his creditors, and paid each one of them not only the entire principal he owed him, but full interest on it beside.

Thomas Symington went to Baltimore, Maryland, where he became a dealer in marble. His success and standing in this enterprise are demonstrated by the fact that it was he who supplied the monolithic columns for the Capitol at Washington, when the additions of the 1850s were made.

One of his business associates was William Steuart, a stone contractor and builder, who as a lieutenant colonel had fought in the defense of Baltimore in 1814, when Francis Scott Key, during the bombardment of Fort McHenry by the British fleet, was inspired to write "The Star-Spangled Banner." So highly regarded was Steuart that he had been elected city councilman, state legislator, and finally mayor of Baltimore.

Thomas Symington married a charming daughter of William Steuart's, named Angeline, thus bringing the name into the family. The couple had four sons and two daughters, of whom there are today more than two hundred descendants, a handsome breed, very highly regarded in Maryland and wherever they have gone.

The eldest son was name William Stuart Symington—after his fighting grandfather, but with the "e" dropped from the Steuart, in the more usual Scottish spelling of the name. A son in each generation since has borne that name.

The first William Stuart Symington was the present Senator's grandfather. He believed wholeheartedly in States' rights, and at the beginning of the Civil War joined the Confederate army. By soldierly merit he attained the rank of major, serving on the staff of General Robert E. Lee, and also of General George E. Pickett. He took part in the futile but heroic Pickett's Charge at the Battle of Gettysburg, the most famous charge in all American history, and was cited for conspicuous gallantry in it. When Lee surrendered at Appomattox, Major Symington gave up his sword with the rest of the decimated Confederate army.

War had wiped out his property and he was a poor man, *very* poor, when he re-entered civilian life. He never was able to recoup his fortunes, and appears to have had an unfortunate business venture that ruined him after he made something of a comeback.

The Major married after the war, and there were seven children born to him by his wife. Then, to complicate matters, she died at a comparatively early age, and he was left with the responsibilities of his household as well as his business cares. The family lived in extreme poverty, but in some manner the sons all received an education.

The Senator's father, the second William Stuart Symington, was born February 6, 1871. He grew up to be a tall, handsome young man, brilliant athletically and intellectually. He attended Johns Hopkins University, was captain of the football team and played on the lacrosse team. He was also a Phi Beta Kappa.

Senator Symington had an interesting hark-back to his father's youth very recently. About 1889, his grandmother took in a youngster who had no money, and boarded him in her house free, in return for which he tutored her children in mathematics, and particularly the Senator's father.

Not long ago Congressman Vaughan Gary, of Richmond, Virginia, came to him and said, "Stuart, funny thing. There's an old teacher, a retired teacher, down in Richmond, who said to me the other day, 'That Senator from Missouri, that Stuart Symington, he has the same name of a lovely lady who boarded me one year in Baltimore for teaching her son.' "

"This is simply fascinating!" exclaimed Symington, who knew the story.

At once he wrote to the old man, whose name was Professor Raines, telling him that he had heard the story many times from his father, and expressing his own gratitude. He received back a warm letter from the old man's daughter, saying that her father was so old, being ninety-seven, that he "thought he had better not write because he had not been feeling well." She added that he had been a teacher for seventy years.

The Senator would have visited him, but very shortly afterward old Professor Raines died. The incident deeply touched Symington, because it was a link with his father and his grandmother.

His father was scholarly and idealistic by nature. Instead of going into business, where his brothers were destined to do extremely well, he chose teaching for his profession, and took his Ph.D. degree in French folklore.

The oldest brother of the family had held a position with the Atlantic Coastline Railroad, after taking a mechanical engineering course at Lehigh University, and when quite young he invented a method of making journal boxes—the boxes which hold and lubricate axles of the wheels on railroad freight cars—and borrowed some money to manufacture these indispensable articles in his own plant.

"They made money," relates the Senator, "but my father stayed out of that business because he was a romanticist and a scholar, and abhorred anything about making money."

This was all very well for him, until he began having a family. His first teaching position was at Stanford University, in California, as an associate professor of Romance languages. He was twenty-three years old when he took it, and according to family tradition, he was so young-looking that the Stanford authorities put a clause into his contract to the effect that he had to grow a beard with which to impress his students.

A year later, in 1895, he was called to a full professorship in Romance languages at Amherst College, Massachusetts. Whether or not he abandoned the contractual beard when he made this change is not of record; but it seems likely, for he persuaded beautiful Emily Harrison to marry him on November 17, 1897.

The new Mrs. Symington, whose father also had fought in the Confederate army, was by all accounts a very remarkable woman. She was of the Virginia Harrisons, a famous family. One of her ancestors, Benjamin Harrison, was a member of the Continental Congress during the Revolutionary War, and a signer of the Declaration of Independence, besides serving three terms as Governor of Virginia. Others of her relatives were William Henry Harrison, hero of the Battle of Tippecanoe, and the ninth President of the United States; and Benjamin Harrison, the twenty-second President.

But like her husband's branch of the Symingtons, her branch of the Harrisons was financially ruined by the Civil War, and the bride brought to her marriage only her rare beauty, a high sense of historical values and responsibilities, and some fine antique furniture.

There was a daughter born to the couple. And then, on June 26, 1901, came the first of five sons. He was christened William Stuart Symington, the third to bear the name, and the circumstance that his father was teaching at Amherst brought about the fact that this member of a Maryland family is a native son of Massachusetts.

Later, the future Senator was to name his eldest son William Stuart Symington IV. But both the Senator and his son, now a successful lawyer in St. Louis, long since dropped the

William from their name. Stuart is Scottish and so is Symington. For a time the Senator signed himself W. Stuart Symington, but he now calls himself simply Stuart Symington, as
does his son, a name shorter and distinctive.

3

The Symington family at Amherst lived in very impecunious
circumstances on the professor's salary, and after five years of
it, the father saw that he could not support his growing family
on it.

One of the family stories, which the Senator delights to
tell, is how the separation from the Massachusetts college
came about. It appears that there was an overbearing and
impudent head janitor at Amherst, who may have been slightly
addicted to the bottle, which would be the only explanation
of the incident as related. One day the janitor came into
Professor Symington's classroom and made some remarks
intended to be humorous which destroyed the atmosphere of
the lecture room and broke up the attention of the class.

The professor—as tall and athletic as is his son—requested
that the man leave the room. The janitor suggested that the
professor try to put him out. This the young professor proceeded to do, first knocking the interloper down, and then
throwing him out.

Inevitably, of course, the affair came before the governing
board of the college. When the hearing was finished, the
officials said very regretfully, "Professor Symington, you have
done excellent work as a teacher. But this janitor with whom
you had trouble is the only man in sixty years who has been
able to keep Amherst College warm in the winter." To that

kind of an alternative there could be but one answer. Professor Symington resigned from Amherst.

Whether this family legend is apocryphal or not, it is true that in 1903 the former teacher turned to the study of law. He chose the law school of New York University, and installed his growing family in a small house in Flushing while he studied.

Those were days of near starvation. He had a tiny savings fund from his teaching career, and he sat up late into the nights doing translation work to augument the small funds from which came the necessities of life. In the summers he sometimes worked in his brothers' plant at Rochester, New York. Yet he succeeded in going through law school, and after another course at Johns Hopkins, obtained entrance to the Maryland bar. But even after he went into practice, the family which grew to include six children, five of them boys, had very little to live on, because the law practice grew slowly.

It did grow over the years, however, and he ended his life as Judge Symington. After his death, February 19, 1926, his friend, Governor Albert C. Ritchie of Maryland, said in a eulogy: "In every fiber of his makeup he always rang perfectly true, and his whole life, I think, was a challenge to anything not completely clean and square and straight."

One of his greatest assets in the period of shabby poverty his family underwent, was his wife. Emily Symington brought up her children in the Episcopal Church, of which she was a devout member, and she gave them not only sincere Christianity, but a sense of honor and conscience, and an unwavering devotion to the country to which they owed their birth. It was from her that Stuart Symington got a start toward that strong feeling for social justice which is today a part of him.

Of a Virginia family which in the past had owned slaves

on its plantation, Symington's mother devoted most of her life to winning full rights for Negroes. She was one of the leaders in Baltimore in the long fight for women's suffrage, and once took part in the picketing of the White House by women for that cause. There is still extant a prayer written by her, which was given at the time the Federal Suffrage Amendment was before the states for ratification:

O Holy Spirit, Fountain of Justice and Love, without which Thy Kingdom cannot come upon earth, pour into the hearts of those in whose power rests the ratification of the Federal Suffrage Amendment such a measure of Thy Love and vision of Thy Justice as may incline them in this gallant undertaking.

Stir up, we beseech Thee, O Lord, the conscience of the nation to a greater sense of its stewardship in the use of the ballot, and to the grave responsibility of withholding it from those who wish to use it in Thy service.

Fill our hearts with joy and thankfulness for success in other states, and to those still striving for this end grant courage with endurance, zeal with wisdom, patient without bitterness.

And grant, O Heavenly Father, that women entering this new field of Service may, in gratitude to Thee, so labor for Thy glory that a Memorial of Thine Abundant Kindness shall be shown. Through Jesus Christ, Our Lord, Amen.

Courage with endurance, zeal with wisdom, patience without bitterness. Stuart Symington keeps that prayer as a remembrance of a brave and beautiful woman, his mother, who believed in her Nation, and in justice for all, and was willing to do her part for it.

All of the six children were bright and handsome. But the most gifted of them, according to his own brothers and sister, was Stuart. It is a family story that in those early days whenever a prize for some sort of attainment was offered the young Symingtons, it was always won by Stuart. Once their mother offered a tennis racket, to be awarded at the end of the summer to the one who best memorized a certain psalm in the Bible. The brother next to him said, "Please Mama, give it to Stuart now, so we can have it to play tennis all summer."

He was a wonderfully handsome child—with very light, almost white hair, and large blue eyes—as well as being a bright child, and it was perhaps natural that he became a little spoiled.

He was an omnivorous reader—at the age of ten he asked for, and received, a set of *Encyclopaedia Britannica* for his Christmas present—and he liked to parade his knowledge. There is a picture of him, taken at the age of six, when his family at a party dressed him in a cap and gown as "The Professor," because of his avid reading.

He was positive in his opinions, sometimes too positive for his age, and there were occasions when he even had arguments with his father at the table, and was sternly ordered to leave it for being too fervent in his opinions which differed from those of his sire, a Ph.D. and an LL.D., as well as very much his senior in age and wisdom.

The father, however, loved and was proud of the brilliant son. He made a habit of not answering the questions with which Stuart constantly showered him, directing him to go and look it up for himself, on the theory that knowledge thus gained made a deeper and more lasting impression than information which was more easily acquired. He thus ingrained in his young son a habit that turned the boy into a tremendous researcher and analyzer in the problems and questions that have confronted him in his lifetime since.

Even in his earlier days the youthful Stuart Symington was by nature exploring, daring, and venturesome, and when he was seven years old he almost lost his life as a result of this.

A horse-drawn delivery truck, loaded with groceries, came to his house one day, and the boy jumped on the back of the vehicle. It took him on a long ride away from home—probably a mile.

There he left the wagon, and while he was walking back, he found some boys playing in a house which was under construction. Some of the boys began jumping from plank to plank, and making dares. Stuart Symington was one of the smaller lads in the group, but he was game. They were on the third story of the half-built house, when one of the larger boys leaped across a rather wide space from joist to joist, there being no flooring laid as yet.

"Dare you to jump that!" he said.

Without hesitation Stuart Symington made the attempt.

His short legs did not carry him far enough. Down he plunged, feet first, through empty space.

Almost certainly the three-story fall would have killed him, had it not been that his left arm, which he flung out, struck over a crossbeam on the way down. It smashed the elbow of the arm, but it broke the fall so that he lived.

The arm healed, but it stiffened. The boy was naturally left-handed, and in the months that followed with a determination remarkable in so young a lad, he set out to make that arm useful. Day after day he exercised it in various ways. Meantime, he taught himself to write with his right hand; he still has the ability to write with either hand. But eventually the left arm was so well rehabilitated that he could play tennis with it—he was a left-handed tennis player—and became a high-class competitor in the sport.

As a footnote to this, when later in life Symington gave up tennis for golf, he studied the game and decided it was designed for right-handed players. The fairways were laid out that way, the dog-legs were designed for the right-handed golfer, and also the traps and approaches to the greens. He thereupon set out to learn the game *right-handed*, and so plays it, and with great proficiency today.

In the early days, while his fathers' law practice seemed to be all "practice" and no returns, the exchequer of the family sometimes ran so low that some of the children were "farmed out" to more prosperous relatives for shorter or longer periods. On at least one occasion Stuart was sent to relatives down in Virginia. His observation as a small boy of the amenities available to people with at least a moderate degree of prosperity, when contrasted with his own home and its Spartan simplicity, gave him a determination very early in life to reach a position of that kind himself, some day.

His cousins went to exclusive private schools, but Stuart and his brothers attended public schools. Once his mother scraped up enough money, or obtained a scholarship in some manner, with which to send him to the Gilman Country School for Boys, in Baltimore. But the amount she managed to get together was barely enough to pay the tuition, and left nothing over for clothing. So her son was sent off to school barefoot, to attend classes with boys who not only were well shod, but well dressed in other ways, since their families could afford it.

This private school lasted only one year, and Stuart went back to public schools. It is the only small bit of fact on which his later political opponent could hang the statement in attempting to fasten the "snobbery" label on him, that "he was educated in exclusive private schools."

Stuart Symington is a product of the public schools, and is proud of it. Furthermore, he is grateful to his teachers in the public schools, for what they did for him. And his recollection of that, and his knowledge of how little they were paid, and how his own father almost starved on a pedagogue's salary, gave him a lifelong resentment against the poor rewards teachers get.

He is a passionate believer in education. Recently, in a speech, he said, "Because, in the end, the brain is our mightiest weapon—mightier by far than the atom—I believe that we have an ever-increasing responsibility to develop our schools and our colleges to the highest possible level, raising our standards, improving our techniques." And that includes, to his mind, paying good teachers sufficiently well to make the profession of teaching attractive to those gifted at it.

It should be added here that when he himself was in grammar school, although he got fine marks, he was, because of his somewhat precocious store of knowledge, inclined to be "self-assured, dogmatic, and sometimes disdainful." It did not, in that stage of his life, make him popular with all his fellows, and it required a few years of age and experience before he gained the tolerance, tact, and humility which characterize his approach to others now, whether it be in social conversation, in an administrative decision, in a Senate debate, or in a free-swinging political campaign.

V

THE FORMATIVE YEARS

1

Even while he was attending grammar school, Stuart Symington was always in the market for odd jobs. His expedients
for earning a little money to help out the family budget were
varied.

One was that typical boyhood enterprise, a paper route.
Quite early in his childhood he exhibited the instinct of a
small entrepreneur, trained his dog to pull his little wooden
wagon, and sold bottled water from house to house in the
neighborhood. He ran errands and mowed lawns.

In June 1912, when he was ten years old, he got his first
smell of politics. That was the year the Democratic National
Convention was held in the Fifth Regiment Armory, in Baltimore. The boy lived just five blocks from the armory, and
there was a neighborhood store they all patronized and called
Miss Linnie's. He got a basket, and he would go to Miss
Linnine's and get it filled, and then he would go to the
armory, and walk through the aisles, crying, "Cigars, cigarettes,
peanuts, chewing gum, chocolates, crackerjacks," to the delegates. He got a percentage on what he sold.

That was the scene of the bitter fight between Woodrow

Wilson and Champ Clark, and it caught his boyish imagination.

"I watched William Jennings Bryan try to get the platform and get it—and watched the boys jump on him to try to prevent it," he says. "It was all very exciting to me. And when Woodrow Wilson was nominated, I rushed down to Miss Linnie's where another boy, Beverly Smith, who is now Washington editor of the *Saturday Evening Post*, was getting his basket filled. And I yelled, 'Wilson has been elected umaniously!' Later on Beverly wrote about the incident in the *Saturday Evening Post*, and commented humorously, 'I knew "umaniously" was wrong, so I felt important.' But that was my first experience in politics."

When he was fourteen, he worked a full summer as an office boy at two dollars a week. The next year, at fifteen, he became an apprentice in a machine shop, at the munificent stipend of six dollars a week.

With all these activities, however, he had time to devote to the natural and normal boy's interest in athletics. He played sand-lot baseball, lacrosse and other games. He also got into a normal amount of mischief.

It was, in fact, during the lacrosse period, when he was sixteen, that the episode of the joy ride in the "borrowed" automobile took place, in which he broke an arm, and which later was revived to be used as a weapon against him in his first Senate race.

It was a typical boyish escapade. Four boys, all members of the same team, were returning from a game to the Symington house. Next door lived a pleasant neighbor, Harry Dorsey Watts, one of the elder Symington's closest friends. Mr. Watts had just bought a new automobile. Cars were still somewhat of a novelty in that day, and this one was expensive for the time, having cost the owner $2,500. Boylike, the four youths went over and examined the shining, mechanical marvel.

One of them—not Symington—seated himself behind the wheel and noticed the keys were still in the ignition lock.

"Let's take a little ride," he suggested.

To the others, it seemed like a good idea at the time. Someone cranked up the car, they all piled in and the "driver" —who knew nothing about driving—unsteadily piloted the machine down the street. Unhappily the venturesome boy at the wheel, trying to go around a corner, overturned the car in a ditch and wrecked it. Symington came out of the accident with a broken right arm.

Police arrived at the scene, and the four crestfallen boys were conducted to the police station, Symington holding his broken arm. They were find $25 apiece for "tampering with an automobile."

The elder Symington paid his son's fine, gave the boy a stern lecture, and also got the parents of the other boys together, to pay for the damage to the car.

In actuality the police were interested chiefly in finding out who really took and drove the car. The charge against him would have been more serious, and the other boys, including Stuart Symington would have gotten off free. But none of the boys would tell, so all of them were given fines.

Later the police went to the elder Symington and said that if his son would tell who drove the car, "he's out, and so are the other two boys."

But the elder Symington refused to ask his son to turn against his friend. In fact he went farther. "On that basis," he told the lad, "the other boy might get into more serious trouble. You'll stand together with your friends."

The case would not even have entered in court records, had it not been that after fining the boys, the case was reopened against them under a different charge, an old Maryland law which made a misdemeanor of "using a cow, horse, vehicle or other personal property" without the owner's permission. The four boys were declared guilty of this archaic law, and paroled to their parents—that being the object of the new prosecution.

"That made my father very angry," Symington recalls. "He said it was double jeopardy. So he appealed the case."

The higher court ruled that since there was no sentence, no further action was needed, and so the case ended, but it became a matter of record.

Meantime Harry Dorsey Watts, the man who owned the car, was as furious over the prosecution as was the elder Symington.

"He was wild—to have the charges withdrawn," the Senator recalls with a smile.

Nobody, Mr. Watts least of all, dreamed of accusing the boys of any thought of keeping, or selling, or even failing to return the car, had not the accident occurred. It was strictly a neighborhood joy ride, and Mr. Watts, who knew every one of the lads and their parents, was as fully aware of it as anybody. But the thing was out of his hands.

Later, however, Mr. Watts had the satisfaction of setting everything straight when by innuendo Symington was accused of having stolen a car, during his first Senatorial campaign. As soon as he learned of it, he wrote the letter which has already been quoted.

2

Aside from that brief episode, Stuart Symington was too busy to get into trouble. With his usual intensity and willingness to sacrifice for an end, he became, and still is, a superior athlete.

The United States had gone to war with the Kaiser's Germany in 1917, and in the summer of 1918, when he finished high school, Symington was 17 years old. The minimum age for accepting volunteers in World War I was eighteen, but in his desire to get into the service, he fabricated slightly for one of the few times in his life, told a recruiting officer he was eighteen, and donned a uniform.

That he was marked for superior things was indicated when he was selected to attend an Officers' Training Camp at Plattsburg, and came out of it a second lieutenant of artillery, the youngest commissioned officer in the American army. But the war ended before he had a chance to see active service. It ended, in fact, while he was still seventeen, before he had reached the actual theoretical age at which he could join the army.

The army very probably had a good effect on him, as it has on most boys. It taught him responsibility, and gave him discipline and a knowledge of organization, and of men. He had before this gotten over his childish cockiness, and was willing to listen to others.

When he was released from the army, he wanted to go to college, and the school he chose was Yale. The family fortunes had improved somewhat, and his father was able to help him a little. But throughout his college career he worked to finance himself. In the summers he had a job as a cub reporter on the

Baltimore Sun, covering sports for two years, and politics one. He became acquainted with Henry L. Mencken and Frank Kent among others, and enjoyed the work. But he did not make enough at it to pay his way fully, so he borrowed from relatives to continue in school.

Where he had not been entirely popular in grammar school, he by now had so well adjusted himself that at Yale he was highly popular. He was handsome, carried his blond head high, liked people, and in turn was liked by them. On the campus, in the varied extracurricular activities of the university, he was a success. He played on the tennis team, which he insists was the best tennis team Yale ever had, was assistant editor of the *Yale News*, belonged to the dramatic society, and made Deke and Elihu societies.

He had a roommate who lived in Washington, D.C., and invited him to come and see him. Out of that came a most important turning point in Stuart Symington's life.

3

The summer of 1921 between his junior and senior years in college, he went over to Washington to see his friend, and the two of them went to a party together. Symington liked parties and pretty girls, but he did not suspect how very important this particular party, or one particularly pretty girl, were going to be for him.

The girl he met at the party was Evelyn Wadsworth, a little younger than he, and so lovely she took his breath away. He had a first impression of blonde hair, wonderful blue eyes, and a stunning smile. Then he danced with her once or twice, and found she had many other things in addition to the extraordinary beauty that everyone who had ever seen her agreed that she possessed. She was witty, and cute, and vivacious. And when they had a few moments for conversation alone, he discovered that she had a mind as brilliant as her appearance, one that won his immediate respect, as she had won his immediate admiration.

At the end of the evening Stuart Symington timidly asked her for a date, and got it. More than probably he went home in something of a daze, because he was deeply in love, something that had never happened to him before. A young man, under such circumstances, can be forgiven for having a roseate image of the girl of his heart. But not many young men have the experience of finding that the girl is to prove over the years even more wonderful than those first imaginings pictured her, as Evelyn Wadsworth was to prove to be.

He went home and considered the matter. He had learned enough about the fascinating girl to know that it was something like presumption for him even to think of her. She was from a patrician New York family, and her father was Senator James W. Wadsworth, a mighty power in the Republican party, an intimate of Henry Cabot Lodge, Charles Evans Hughes, Elihu Root and others, a man seriously considered as a Presidential possibility, and immensely wealthy as well.

What could a poor young man, with nothing in his favor except a dead-earnest determination to get along in life, offer to a girl from a family like that?

He could do one thing: he could find out.

The "faint heart that ne'er won fair lady" was not Stuart Symington's.

And so, in a $14 suit, he took the train over from Baltimore, and then a street car, and went up to 800 Sixteenth Street, to the Hay-Adams house across the street from the White

House, to claim his date. The upshot was somewhat embarrassing and amusing.

"It was a mighty big house for a little boy from Baltimore who used to be sent down to his relatives in Virginia," he recalls. "I rang the bell. The butler answered it. I'd never seen a Senator and I'd never seen a butler in a dress suit. So when a great big impressive looking man came to the door, I stuck out my hand and said, 'How do you do, Senator?' It must have set me back with her folks for a year."

But perhaps it wasn't as bad as that. There is pretty good evidence that Senator Wadsworth liked the young man who came to call on his daughter from the very first, even though they differed rather sharply in politics. Alden Hatch, in his biography of Senator Wadsworth, *The Wadsworths of Genesee*, puts it this way:

> Senator Wadsworth had watched his daughter's romance benignly. He liked the young man immensely, though they had some pretty hot political arguments. The fact that his daughter's best beau would not yes him on political principles made the Senator feel fine about the whole thing.

Stuart Symington returned that regard, with interest. It is not too much to say that Senator Wadsworth, in spite of the fact that they were poles apart politically, became his first and greatest hero; and perhaps still remains so long after his death. Today he frequently speaks of his wife's father with affection and reverence, and relates words of wisdom and guidance he received from him. After Senator Wadsworth's death, he uttered this sincerest of tributes:

"In a general way, Senator Wadsworth's most important contribution to government was character. He was so far above party that both sides trusted him. In England it is an honor to be in politics; over here many people regard it as an undesirable effort. A man of the character and following of Senator Wadsworth raises the plane of all government. He did not have integrity; he *was* integrity."

In the meantime, what about the young lady who was so deeply concerned? It is quite probable that Evelyn Wadsworth knew the kind of a young man she wanted when she saw him, and also perhaps with feminine intuition sensed the kind of a man he would become as time passed. The young folks came to an understanding, and began making plans to be married.

When their engagement was announced, in 1923, Senator Wadsworth wrote to a friend:

> Alice [Mrs. Alice Hay Wadsworth] and I are very happy about it. Young Symington is the kind of a man who looks you straight in the eye.

4

The romance had more to it than love and marriage, important as they are. It completely and unalterably changed the course and tenor of Stuart Symington's life.

Long before he went to college he had intended to be a lawyer like his father; and he probably would have made a great lawyer. But now, all at once, the most important thing in the world to him was to be somewhere near the girl he was to marry.

Evelyn Wadsworth's family home was in Geneseo, New York, where since Revolutionary times the Wadsworths had been large land-owners, Originally their land had been purchased from the Iroquois Indians. They developed it into rich farms and made it prosper, and built upon it the family mansion, a house based on the plans of an English friend, Lord Hertford, for his villa in Regent's Park. It came close to being called "the Long House," which was the name the Iroquois had for their great primitive residence, but instead was named for the English villa, Hartford House, the spelling somewhat changed to agree with the British pronunciation of Hertford.

The T. H. Symington Company, later the Symington-Gould Company, where his uncles made journal boxes and other heavy railroad equipment, was located at Rochester, New York, only twenty-five or thirty miles from Geneseo. That probably was the impelling reason why Stuart Symington went there and asked for a job.

He asked for a job, not a "situation," and he got just that —a job. They put him on the payroll as an apprentice molder, which meant heavy labor and long hours. A molder in an iron works forms molds in a mixture of sand and clay, and then pours into it molten iron to solidify in the shapes required. He works often in stifling heat, in dust and smoke, and at backbreaking toil. Symington rose early, by the alarm clock, to be on the job at seven o'clock in the morning. He worked long hours, boarded as cheaply as he could, and often had for lunch only a bottle of milk and a piece of apple pie. But he kept at it and presently he was a full-fledged journeyman molder.

He went to work in June 1923, and whenever he could save enough money and take the time off, he would go down to visit his girl. Hard as his work was, he had his usual enthusiasm for what he was doing, and also he was beginning to get his first real insight into the problems and aspirations and troubles of men who worked with their hands for a living. That was something he and the girl talked about, too.

"I got to know people on that job," he says. "There weren't any unions. When I went to Rochester the shipping foreman was a Negro, an incredibly advanced man. In the South things were a little different and you didn't see colored men in such positions, but I got to knowing that man and respecting him and liking him for his ability and character, and it opened up a new world to me that I've never forgotten: that Negroes are the same as white people, some good, some bad, some with ability, some not, but people with people's feelings and problems and hopes and disappointments.

"Another man, the yard foreman, asked me to come to dinner with him. We would go there and he would have to go upstairs to carry his wife down. She was a hopeless cripple and he took care of her and the house and worked.

"One poor fellow was bitter against prohibition. He said he came from a 'good family' and had come down in the world, and was discouraged. 'Now my only release is to get drunk on Saturday night,' he told me. And prohibition had taken that prop from him. You maybe didn't respect something like that, but you couldn't help sympathizing with it. It was another side of the picture.

"Then I knew a man who went to bed every night at five-thirty or six o'clock. He got up at one o'clock in the morning, and didn't bother his family. He went down to an all-night lunchroom, ate, then got on a street car and rode an hour, got to work about four o'clock in the morning—on piece work—and worked until four o'clock the next afternoon, twelve hours every day of his life, on piece work.

"And then this man got on a street car and went home and was in bed by six o'clock every night of his life. When I asked him, 'Why do you live this way?' he said, 'I've got two children, a son and a daughter, in the Eastman School of Music, and this is the only way I can pay the bills.'

"Now, when you hear that kind of stuff, you're just ashamed.

And having dealt with those people, it got to be a part of my background.

"Why, the greatest lady I ever knew in my life, bar none, was the first woman who ever boarded me. Her house, way up on a little side street in Rochester, had only one bathroom. She and her husband, very nice but not much good at making a living, and two daughters and a deaf mute lived there, besides me. One of the daughters taught in a deaf-mute institute.

"I tell you, this woman was the most magnificent woman that the world could know. I lived with her, $10 a week, room and board, and the finest food I have eaten. My roommate was Jack Kellogg, who later married the daughter of the head of the Continental Illinois Trust in Chicago. We used to get up in the morning—we had to get to work by seven o'clock, and it was a mess. We had an old Essex four.

"Once when we couldn't get it started we rode to work in a taxicab. That was way beyond those poor Italians, and Portuguese, and Spaniards, and other fellows that were in the molding business. They couldn't believe their eyes. They would never take a taxi in their life—they would walk twenty miles instead. But that's how we got to work that time. And I worked hard, too.

"Anyway, I went through all that. And it was like heaven when I could wash up good and go down to the Genesee Valley."

VI

THE GIRL OF
THE GENESEE VALLEY

1

"The Valley of the Genesee" meant Evelyn Wadsworth, who is known to all who are close to her as Eve. The couple was much in love, and presently they decided that even though he was working in a foundry, and it might be some time before he got a position with a good salary, there was no reason why they should wait any longer to be married.

So it was arranged, and Stuart Symington took time off, and went to Washington, and there he and Eve Wadsworth were married, in Senator Wadsworth's home, March 1, 1924, in a brilliant society wedding, at which President and Mrs. Calvin Coolidge were among the guests present.

From all that splendor, the bride and groom went to a two-room apartment in Rochester, and began to keep house. The new Mrs. Stuart Symington was having some novel experiences. For example, her young husband, working as a molder, came home at nights so covered with sand, grime, and sweat, that "it took two baths to remove the smudge each evening." Furthermore, she found that in her husband she had no skylarking playmate. He had by this time a definite goal in view.

He was going to get to the top, and it required study. As always, he was playing to win.

She cooked their meals—incidentally, she still likes to cook for them. After supper Symington would get out his books and bone up, or attend night school classes in mechanical and electrical engineering. One course he took at night school was mathematics, the subject in which he had been poorest at college. And he subscribed to and took a correspondence course in metallurgy from the International Correspondence School.

As a footnote, to illustrate the nature of the man, in Stuart Symington's *Who's Who* biography, he lists that correspondence school as an alma mater, right along with Yale.

Some brides might have been disconcerted or disappointed or even resentful, but Eve Symington has a rare and unusual spirit. She was lovely and accomplished and accustomed to every luxury and refinement of life, but not once did she falter or lose patience and understanding during those long two years while he studied furiously to improve himself.

The girl from the Genesee Valley was as much a thoroughbred as her husband, and they complemented and supplemented each other with qualities the other respected, admired, and cherished.

Her background of family extends even farther back than that of the Symingtons. The first Wadsworth, indeed, landed at Boston in 1632.

The family has been noted throughout its long career for public service, beginning back in the troublous Colonial period. History generally credits a Wadsworth—Captain Joseph Wadsworth—with the first act of rebellion by an American colonist against the British crown. It occurred in 1687, when the tyrannical Royal Governor, Sir Edmund Andros, sought to revoke the charter given to Connecticut by King Charles II.

The charter was on the table in the Hartford meeting house, and the Governor was advancing to take it up, when suddenly all the candles in the room were snuffed. There was confused movement, and when the candles were lit again, the precious charter, guarantee of the liberties and rights of the colonists, was gone.

Later, when the danger of its seizure and revocation was past, it was "discovered" in the hollow of an oak tree where Captain Wadsworth had secreted it. The tree was always called Charter Oak, and was regarded with reverence, until it fell in 1856, at an estimated age of 1000 years. Captain Wadsworth retained possession of the charter for several years, until it could be safely returned to its accustomed place.

But there were other Wadsworths in the march of American history. Colonel Jeremiah Wadsworth was a personal friend of George Washington's, and served as Commissary General of the Continental Army. James Wadsworth was the first to dare the fierce Iroquois and acquire the land from them now is the Genesee Valley. General William Wadsworth fought in the War of 1812, and was wounded at the Battle of Queenstown Heights. General James S. Wadsworth was killed at the Battle of the Wilderness in the Civil War, leading a Union corps which included the famed Iron Brigade.

Eve Symington's grandfather, James Walcott Wadsworth, was a Congressman, and her father, James Walcott Wadsworth, Jr., was the Senator from New York.

Her mother was the former Alice Hay, daughter of John Hay, who was Lincoln's private secretary and biographer, and Secretary of State under McKinley. One of her grandmothers was Marie Louisa Travers, daughter of William R. Travers, a crony of Joseph Choate and Chauncey Depew; and granddaughter of Reverdy Johnson of Baltimore, who was Attorney General of the United States, Senator from Maryland, and Minister to the Court of St. James in England.

The young wife had fine blood in her, and she showed it in those trying years. It was the beginning of a devotion between Stuart and Eve Symington that has lasted more than thirty-five years at this writing, the kind of a marriage that is nearly ideal, where each has a bountiful reservoir from which to give to the other, where mutual strength is increased by long living and working together, and where admiration and affection grow with the passing years.

There were some important contributions made by Mrs. Symington in those days. One of her husband's defects then was a rather incandescent temper. On occasion he would "blow his top," as the saying goes—spectacularly, and not always wisely. But she was serene and tactful, and she understood him and she could often quiet his hot anger and show him how to do things in a more diplomatic fashion. Give Eve Symington a good share of the credit for the way that her husband has learned to control his temper, even in the face of manifest wrong and malice. The temper is still there, but it is a controlled anger now, and becomes purposeful.

2

In the midst of the almost ascetic drive for the kind of training he needed, Symington's wife presented him, June 12, 1925, with their first child, a little boy who was promptly christened William Stuart Symington IV. The arrival of a grandson pleased Senator Wadsworth mightily. He wrote twinklingly to a friend:

It was very good of you to send me a note of congratulations. The grandson and his mother are doing splendidly. It is uncertain what the boy's political affiliations will be. His father is a Maryland Democrat. I am a little disturbed by this.

The following year Senator Wadsworth taught his son-in-law a lesson in devotion to the service of the nation. In 1926 he was defeated for re-election as Senator, because he refused to "vote dry and drink wet" as so many politicians were doing in that day when the Prohibition Amendment was proving a failure, and permitting the dark forces of the underworld to amass vast fortunes which have kept the crime experts going ever since.

It did not embitter the man who had been in the Upper House of the Nation's Congress since 1915. He did not give up working in politics, and later stood for office as a Congressman, which many would have considered a demotion. Furthermore, he was elected, and continued to represent his district in the Lower House until his retirement in 1950.

Another great family of public servants, the Adams family, had set a precedent for this when John Quincy Adams, after being defeated by Andrew Jackson when he ran for a second term as President, ran for Congress, and kept his seat in it until his death. Both these men did what they did "for the good of the country."

Stuart Symington never forgot that lesson in selflessness.

For the present, however, he was too busy to delve very deeply into politics. He and Eve were the delighted parents of a second son, whom they named James Wadsworth Symington, for his grandfather, the Senator, on September 28, 1927.

The youthful father was a tall young man with ambitions

equally tall, and his wife and two little sons made him even more eager to get ahead.

He had not studied hard and long for nothing, and he could spot defects in methods and techniques, which he did not hesitate to express. One day he told the heads of the company that a car coupler they were making at one of their subsidiary plants was "a louse because we can't pour iron right."

He was promptly fired.

But events proved him right. He was rehired, and given a job at a drafting board. This he disliked.

Next he made an essay on his own. He had found a clay which bonded well with sand, and he spent a year selling this high-bond clay to foundries for molding.

Then the family business took him in again, to head their lighting and battery plant. He inspected it, and told the head of the company that there was nobody on the lot who knew how to make batteries.

Again he was fired.

This time he went on his own for good. He began making radio loudspeakers under the name of Valley Appliances, Inc., at Rochester. After the 1929 stock market crash, came the Depression and businesses were falling like tenpins. The radio market went to pieces along with almost everything else.

Instead of being alarmed, however, Symington studied the market and looked around him. Because speakers began to move into consoles, he either had to get into the set business, or out of the radio business. He saw a chance to acquire a set manufacturing company by way of a merger, but he needed money. He knew someone who had it—his uncles. So he went to them, and persuaded them to back him in acquiring the Colonial Radio Corporation.

It was the first of a series of impressive demonstrations of victory by an amazing personality. But the more impressive part of it was the performance afterward.

The history of Symington's achievements is always divided into three parts: the conception, when he plans out his idea; the exercise of his remarkable personality in selling the idea; and always the execution afterward, whereby he proves that the conception and the persuasion were sound.

In this case, he needed a market. Accordingly he went to Sears, Roebuck and Company, and made a proposition to General Robert E. Wood, president of that great company. He would take over the company's plant at Buffalo, New York, and operate it in connection with Colonial's plant on Long Island, receive contracts from Sears to purchase merchandise over a period of years, and in return give the company part of the stock in his own firm.

General Wood listened, sized up his man, and said, "All right. I'll take 25 per cent of the stock in return for these contracts."

"No you won't," said Symington. "You'll take 49 per cent."

General Wood looked surprised. "What's this all about?" he asked.

"I want a partner, not a customer," said Symington.

General Wood nodded, with a smile that might have contained a wee bit of admiration and wonder at this persuasive young man's ways of doing things. The whole transaction was another instance of sheer personality . . . and also, it might be said, of foresight.

So there Stuart Symington was, president and a substantial stockholder in a company with a big backlog of orders, including not only radios but cream separators, all contracted at a minimum dollar figure Sears would take each year. And he was at the ripe old age of twenty-nine.

Young? Perhaps. But it made no difference in his case. He had to put his plants into operation and deliver the radio sets as promised, and into this he channeled the same drive, the same intelligent application, that he had put into everything in his life. The competitive instinct in him caused him to meet the hardest problems head-on, as if they were enemies to be overcome.

Times were bad, and sometimes he had to innovate and improvise. But always he seemed to find an expedient, and got things shored up and working. What he lacked in experience he made up for in energy and imagination, and he gained experience fast. His agile and retentive mind grasped at everything, and once he learned something about anything—technique, production, management, sales—he never forgot it.

Under normal conditions he would have prospered well, but the distress market was rampant, radio companies were failing rapidly, and by early summer of 1932 the Depression was at its depth.

In the midst of this Symington went to see General Wood again.

"With things the way they are," he said, "I know you can't sell the merchandise I'm making for you. Therefore, I don't feel that under the terms of the contract, even though Sears is obligated, it is right for me to demand that you take it."

Again General Wood was surprised, and not a little impressed.

For a moment he studied, then he said, "How much money would it take to run your company through the end of this year, 1932, if you have no business at all?"

Symington said that he did not know, but would let the General know next morning. This he did.

General Wood immediately called in his financial vice president and told him to extend to Symington a line of credit for the amount he had named, regardless of any amount of business Sears placed under the contracts. Then turning to Symington, he said, with a twinkle in his eye:

"Don't forget, you wanted a partner, not a customer." And he added, "Times are bad now but I have complete faith in America's future."

Things picked up in 1933 and Symington's enterprise was on its way. He had acquired Colonial in 1930. He built it into one of the most successful enterprises of its kind. By 1935 its value had so increased that when he and his stockholders sold it to Sylvania Products, his equity in it made him his first fortune.

"One thing I was glad about after that wonderful gesture of confidence on General Wood's part," he says today, "was that for the difference between the 25 per cent and 49 per cent of the stock, he received a handsome piece of change when the company was sold."

3

But that is getting a little ahead of the story.

It was in this period, when he was working harder than he ever had in his life, that he had the appelation "playboy" hung on him—undeservedly as will be seen.

Since the Colonial plant was on Long Island, the Symingtons moved down from Rochester to New York. Symington was, however, no playboy. A person has to work at the thing to be a playboy, and in this period he was working, all right, but working night and day at his business.

What really happened was a surprising occurrence that actually was not so surprising after all, if you know the graceful and talented Eve Symington. From the first the pair were in demand socially. They were handsome, well-bred, charming, gay, and young, a delightful asset to any company.

Mrs. Symington became interested in the Belleview Cardiac Committee and its work, and one night she and her husband attended a benefit at the Place Pigalle, a swank night club, given for the Belleview work. She had a musical education, and had sung for friends, and on this night, after the regular professional entertainers had been on, someone suggested that Eve Symington sing.

As a lark, and for the sake of the cause for which the affair was being held, she went to the microphone, looking very lovely under the spotlight, and began to sing in a voice so caressingly rich and low in timbre, that her thrilled listeners gave her an ovation when she finished. Again she sang, several times, and each time received the same mighty applause.

The place was filled with her friends, and while she was grateful for their applause, she did not take it very seriously. To her utter surprise, however, after she finished the management of the club came to her with an offer of a contract to sing professionally during the fall season.

One who was not surprised at her reception was Stuart Symington.

"There she was, with this unbelievable voice, and she was standing with this lovely mass of blonde hair," he says. "She sang where everybody there but her was a pro, and when those pros heard her, they offered her a job. She asked me, and

I said, 'Why not? You do anything in the world you want to. But you'd better ask your father before you decide—he's in politics.' "

Why not, indeed? The idea appealed to her, it was a challenge, and she wanted to do it. But first she telephoned and asked her father. The conversation, as reported, was as follows:

"I'd like to do it," she said, "but will it embarrass you in any way? Degrade or compromise your career?"

There was a short pause, then the Senator asked, "Is it east or west of Broadway?"

"One block east."

"Go ahead," said her father. "I trust you."

She opened up in the fall, billed as "Evie Symington, the Society Singer," at the Place Pigalle. Her debut as a professional singer was tinged with nervousness. Many of her friends were in the audience, and she got plenty of applause, but she was afraid it was only her loyal friends that gave it.

But then she went on, and she was given a storm of applause evening after evening, whether her friends were there or not. She was good. She was very good. She sang at the swankiest places in New York—the Iridium Room of the St. Regis, the Persian Room of the Plaza, and the Sert Room of the Waldorf-Astoria among others. Before she was through she was earning $1,750 a week, and had a really important Hollywood offer.

But it wasn't the money that interested her. She had some money in her own right, and would inherit more. Her husband was doing extremely well. It was the doing of it that intrigued her, the achievement of breaking into the toughest entertainment field in the world, and making a great success of it. She loved it, and the town loved her.

It was while she was singing in night spots in New York that her husband got the "playboy" tag. He was her proud and devoted fan.

"I liked to hear her sing," he says. "I was working hard, but I'd go just as often as I could to where she was. Well, after all, a man likes to see his wife, especially when she's doing such a great job. So I was around a lot, and since she sang in night clubs, that was where I was. I suppose some people thought I didn't have anything else to do, and so it added up to the playboy idea."

That actually is all there was to it: a hard-working young husband, proud and happy over a pretty and talented young wife's success, with a perfectly natural wish to see and applaud her, coming to hear her sing in the fashionable night spots of New York.

4

"Evie Symington, the Society Singer," never forgot that she was a wife and mother. She budgeted her time so that she could devote as much of it as possible to her two boys and her husband.

And everyone she worked with was completely devoted to her. Symington tells a story:

"One night I went to a club to hear her with Gene Tunney, who is my close friend—he and Polly are real friends of Evie and me. Gene looked wonderfully handsome that night. His face was completely unscarred and he had a red flower in his buttonhole. We went to the bar, and suddenly he looked over at one of the barkeepers and said, 'Jack!' And the fellow looked up and said, 'Champ!'" The barkeep was Jack Renault, the old lumberjack fighter, who had fought Gene a terrific battle once, and they were as glad to see each other as a pair of real buddies.

"Gene said, 'Jack, it's good to see you.' And Renault said, 'Oh, my, you look great, Champ.' And then Gene said, 'You know, in that third round you had me worried. I might as well be frank with you.' And Renault grinned, mighty pleased, and said, 'You wouldn't be kidding me, would you, Champ?' Gene said, 'If you'd been just a little quicker in that third round . . .' And they fought that round, and the whole fight over, blow by blow, just as you and I would go over a golf score.

"After a while, Gene introduced me, and told Renault I was Evie Symington's husband. 'Kind of keep an eye on her, will you, Jack?' he said. And Jack Renault said, 'That little lady? She's the queen of the town. There isn't anybody here who wouldn't do anything in the world for her. Why, if anybody got fresh with her or even gave her a wrong look, we'd break him into little bitsy pieces right there on that dance floor!' "

That was the kind of devotion Evie Symington commanded. She was a great lady, and she was treated accordingly by everyone.

That career kept her busy for four years, and naturally she loved it, any woman would have loved it. But a good many women would have had their heads turned by the applause and the flattery and the attention and the success. It has that kind of effect too frequently.

And here is the revealing side of Evelyn Symington, the proof of her exceptional quality. The applause and attention and money did not for one instant turn her head. When, later, it became necessary for her husband to go to St. Louis to live, and to breathe new life into a dying industry, she gave up the career as quickly and gracefully as she had entered it. She canceled every contract, and without a backward look, went to St. Louis with her husband and her family, as soon as she could finish her present obligations.

"She was the toast of New York," says Symington. "There was nobody who could sing a song the way she sang it, or look as wonderful while she sang. And she gave all that up. I called her up from St. Louis, and said, 'In the name of godness, now wait a minute.' She said, 'Well, I've just decided I'm through, and when I'm through, I'm through.' I said, 'You'll get an awful lot of people upset.' And she said, 'All I want is to be a good wife and a good mother from now on.'

"So she didn't sing again. She was just through and she was the greatest. I never heard her sing until our son Jim started to sing—she just quit—just like that. Fortunately I have some records of hers. She was, and is, simply the greatest."

VII

THE EMERGENCY AT EMERSON

1

Stuart Symington has the ability of making friends everywhere, some of whom have had an important bearing on his life. Among those he made in New York was a man with a handsome face in spite of a slightly flattened nose—broken in a college boxing match—and a pleasant, decisive manner. He was James Forrestal, president of the banking firm of Dillon, Read and Company. The careers of Forrestal and Symington were destined to be closely meshed in the future, but neither of them knew it then.

Another friend was Charles Payson, who owned the Rustless Iron and Steel Company in Baltimore. Rustless Iron was in the business doldrums, and Payson watched with interest Symington's spectacular success with Colonial Radio Corporation. When Colonial was sold in 1935, Payson asked Symington if he would not see what he could do about Rustless Iron.

Symington looked the plant over, studied the books, and saw that the problem of resuscitating it offered a considerable challenge. A challenge is something that appeals to him, and so after a brief consideration, he took the job. Furthermore, he showed his belief in himself by accepting as a good part of his compensation an option on a substantial block of stock. If he could put the company back on its feet, he would make money on that stock. If he failed, he would get nothing.

But he had no intention of failing. By this time he had developed a standard program for "doctoring" sick firms. It included having a survey made by a good firm of management engineers, a codification of every fact concerning the business, the issuing of a chart of structure and function so that every man knows his duty and what is expected of him and to whom he reports, and a stern but fair expectation that employees will perform as required, or face discharge. The last gets rid of a lot of deadwood that often gathers about a limping company. "Men don't mind how tough you are," he says, "if they know you're fair and are accomplishing something."

It took him only two years to revitalize Rustless Iron and Steel, expand both its production and its orders, and turn it into a thumping moneymaker. So successful did the company become, indeed, that in 1937 American Rolling Mill bought it at a figure that made Symington's block of stock worth so much that, if he desired, he could retire—at the age of thirty-six.

Now, if he had inclinations in that direction, was the opportunity for him to become a real playboy. He lacked the inclinations.

It is impossible for Stuart Symington to be happy without something creative to do. He cannot relax and grow soft and sluggish. Like a championship athlete he needs something against which he can exercise his strength and skill and brains. He is at his best when he is confronted by a job that people say is impossible, but which he believes can be done if sufficient effort and ability are put into it.

A few months of leisure were quite enough for him. Then he began toying with one or two business ideas, including the manufacture of parking meters—of which more later.

Meantime, in St. Louis, Missouri, there was a company that needed help badly. The Emerson Electric Manufacturing Company of St. Louis was an old firm which had fallen on evil days.

It had, for one thing, the worst possible labor relations, and had just undergone the second longest sit-down strike in history—fifty-three days, during which the men occupied the plant in three shifts a day, played ping-pong and checkers, had impromptu sing-fests, and otherwise whiled away the time while the plant stood idle and unproductive.

Emerson Electric was organized in 1890 to manufacture electric fans, and was named for one of its organizers, Judge J. W. Emerson. For a while it did quite well, and Emerson fans were well known and widely used throughout the summer-heated Midwest, competing successfully with similar products like Westinghouse and General Electric.

From time to time the management changed, and the original formers of the company dropped out or died. After World War I, Emerson expanded its production into other spheres, such as motors, hair driers, and frog switches for street cars, but fans continued to be the big item.

Then came the great depression. Emerson paid its stockholders a dividend in 1930. It was the last dividend paid on common stock and by 1937 even preferred stock had been passed over.

One of the large financial interests in Emerson was held by the investment banking firm of Van Alstyne, Noel and Com-

pany. David Van Alstyne saw that new management was
needed, and began looking for the right man. He had learned
the investment banking business under James Forrestal at
Dillon, Read and Company, and now he went to Forrestal
for advice.

Forrestal gave him the best advice possible: he told him
to get Symington for the job. When Symington was asked to
take charge the company had just succeeded in losing
$117,000 the previous year and the preferred stock dividend
was in arrears. In the long strike the workers had obtained a
five per cent wage increase and a minimum of 32 cents an
hour, but they were sullen and suspicious of anyone in management.

If a tough, hard job was what Symington was looking for,
he was offered it here. So he took it.

2

First he insisted that he should have full powers, and the
stockholders, who had been studying his record, agreed. He
was made president and chairman of the board of Emerson,
and once again, showing his faith in himself, he took an option on 75,000 shares as part of his remuneration. He would
rise or fall by what he did for the company.

Symington took over the plant in 1938. "He is a lanky,
loose-jointed man who canters around with the exuberant
energy of a well-bred horse," one observer wrote at the time.

And a St. Louis matron cried, "Look, his hair is taffy-
colored."

When he arrived, he took rooms at the Racquet Club,
because his wife was still singing, his family was in New
York, and he was not sure how long his stay would be. Then
he went to work.

First he gave the plant a close study. Next he began getting rid of deadwood in the management and seeing that the men who did their work well were suitably promoted. One of these, Oscar C. Schmitt, became executive vice president with a good raise in salary, and a member of the board. Another, John A. Driy, a hard-working engineer, was made operating vice president, and also got a seat on the board. A third was Fred Karches, who became personnel director. Later on, Symington was to alter his stock agreement to make it possible for some of the men in management to buy 25,000 shares of his stock.

There were two great first necessities: new business, and better production. He went out after the first, and got new customers. One of them was Sears, Roebuck and Company, which remembered the satisfactory relations with Symington in the days when he was making Silvertone radios at Colonial.

The second necessity, that of production, was primarily a matter of solving the labor problem, and that, Symington says, is one of the things that first attracted him to Emerson. He was familiar with the United Electric, Radio, and Machine Workers, and had worked on good terms with the union at Colonial. He and the union's president, James B. Carey, understood and respected each other. He had been a laborer himself, and he had a feeling for and sympathy with the problems of the working men and women.

Head of the union in St. Louis was the late William Sentner, a self-proclaimed Communist, but a man who kept his promises. He was suspicious of Symington at the beginning, but as the conferences continued the feeling changed.

Symington began by laying his cards on the table.

"Your wages are too low," he said to the union leaders, "but Emerson can't pay you more at present. Here are the books. Examine them yourselves, and see that I'm telling you the absolute truth. If we begin to show a profit, I'll promise that your wages will go up. In the meantime, as the first step, I'll offer the union a voluntary check-off system." Sentner stared through his glasses in surprise and distrust. He had never heard of an industrialist making such a concession except under great pressure.

"What's the catch?" he asked.

"No catch," said Symington. "I want Emerson to be a good place to work, and if we're going to have a union I want a strong union. This offer is straight, with no strings attached."

A check-off, whereby a union receives dues, fees, fines, and assessments of its members directly from the employer who withholds them from their pay, is of course an arrangement very valuable to the union in its operation.

"You know, I'm beginning to believe in you," said Sentner. "We'll take the check-off. And we'll take the wage increases when you can make them, for every cent we can, right down to the half cent."

"Don't worry, I'll cut your people in," promised Symington. He was as good as his word.

"When I went to Emerson," he says with some pride today, "the average take-home pay was less than sixteen bucks a week. When I left there seven years later, it was just under fifty dollars a week. And nobody profited more by it than I."

3

Not long afterward, the workers at Emerson had a chance to prove their faith in the new operator of the plant. Symington had expanding ideas, and they rallied around him.

"It's necessary to follow the customer in business," he says. "Why is there a Rural Electrification Administration today? Because the power companies wouldn't follow the customer. The rural customer was out there, but they didn't have to go to him, and they were making so much money the easy way, in the congested population centers, that they wouldn't go the hard way. So the REA came into being, to reach the customers the private companies wouldn't.

"That's one thing I always watched in my business. Don't think I was the smartest man in my business. There were buckets of them at Emerson smarter than I was, who knew the business better. But one day I called a meeting and said, 'Why are we losing all this electrical motor business? We're making washing machine motors, what about refrigerator motors?'

"They said to me, 'Refrigerator motors go into hermetics.' I said, 'Well, then, let's go into hermetics.' They replied, 'They're very difficult to make.' 'But,' I said, 'we can't just decide not to make them because it's difficult. We've got to follow the market.' Then they said, 'We'd have to have a new plant to do it, and it would all have to be air-conditioned, and so on.' I said, 'Well, let's build a new plant then.' They objected that we didn't have any money. I said, 'We don't have to have money. Let's go to one of the banks. The banks are loaded up with money.'"

But before he went to a bank he visited Ray Herrick in Tecumseh, Michigan, who was making hermetically sealed motors, to learn something about it.

"The first time I went to see him," relates Symington, "he sent word out that he was too busy. I sent word back in that I wasn't interested in his problems—I wanted to see him and talk about hermetic motors. It must have astonished him, for he came out to see me.

"His first words were, 'Have you got any money and have you got any guts?' I said, 'I've got no money, but I've got plenty of guts.' So he said, 'Well, we'll talk about it.' "

The interview is typical of the airy Symington way of refusing to be brushed off. But it was only one of many inquiries and studies he made on the problem. Among other things he realized that he had to find a site and financial backing for a more suitable plant.

While he grappled with this problem, up-and-coming Evansville, Indiana, sent over a delegation to him, offering him a site and $100,000 for moving expenses, if he would take his plant there. Symington did not wish to leave St. Louis, and it was at this point that the Electrical Workers came to his assistance.

The union held a meeting one day, and after that went to Symington with an offer to put up $40,000 for the new plant, if the city of St. Louis would put up the rest. When the Chamber of Commerce hesitated, for fear of establishing a precedent, the union held another meeting and voted to furnish the entire $100,000 itself, through a self-imposed system of wage cuts.

But Symington had not been idle. He found a suitable site in St. Louis County. And then he went to one of the banks to use his wonderful persuasive power in an effort to arrange financing. It was another story of a personality that creates faith in people. A wise old banker, at the end of the discussion said, "I have no right to lend you this money, Stuart, but I'm going to do it."

So, with the site and financing in hand, Symington thanked the union most sincerely for its offer, and declined the immediate tender of cash, but said he would like to hold the offer open, with the union's consent, so that if he needed it at any time in the next two years he might accept it.

He never called upon the union for its money. Instead, he had carried Emerson so far along the rising path of success in 1940, two years later when the offer came to an end, that he instituted instead a profit-sharing plan for the employees.

4

Long before then, however, he had become a permanent resident of St. Louis. Mrs. Symington, who had closed her last engagement under existing contracts, brought her two young sons, and they all went house hunting.

They bought a pleasant brick house in Creve Coeur, a St. Louis suburb, and at once the family became a popular part of the community.

And this in spite of the fact that some of the businessmen of St. Louis did not see eye to eye with Symington in his labor policies. It was even worse than that. Some of the more conservative industrialists were vocal in their disapproval of his fair attitude toward his employees.

The question was raised as to whether he could remain a member of the Racquet Club, with the kind of ideas he had. "I was nearly ridden out of St. Louis on a rail," Symington grins.

A few of his most vehement critics went so far as to say that he had "sold out" to the union. This puzzled him, for he considered his dealings purely a matter of reciprocal business. As he expressed it to one interviewer, "It's balanced industrial democracy that works: the union gets good wages and working conditions, Emerson gets the cooperation of the employees in better and more production."

To the criticism that he had dealt with "a self-confessed Communist," he merely pointed out the fact that Sentner was the head of the union, and under the law he was required to deal with the head of the union, whatever his politics.

Eventually the union itself threw the Communists out and reorganized as the International Union of Electric Workers. In that battle Symington gave strong help to the anti-Communist movement, and later, in the Senate he sponsored legislation requiring non-Communist affidavits from private institutions and training establishments before they could qualify under the G.I. bill, another measure requiring non-Communist affidavits under the Service Veterans Readjustment Act, and a third for continued investigation of how best to combat the international Communist conspiracy against the United States.

He also supported and voted for the legislation in 1954 to outlaw the Communist party in the United States, "because I believe it is an illegal conspiracy striving to overthrow our government by force and violence."

As to the legitimate union workers there is no question that Symington's advanced ideas of social justice strengthened the electrical workers in other parts of the country. As to Emerson, it began to produce more smoothly and better than ever before, and there were no labor troubles of any kind in the plant during Symington's management.

His "experiment" attracted wide attention, so much so that he was invited to address the Society for the Advancement of Management at its Spring conference, April 11, 1940. It was his first speech, and the occasion was somewhat historic, for in it he first gave utterance to some ideas then called "radical" but now generally accepted as "sound."

He began modestly by saying, "For me to address this society on the question of getting the production job done is like a college player explaining to the Yankee infield how to play ground balls."

But then he spoke with vigor, confidence, and original thought.

"Many centuries ago," he said, "a wise old Greek made the following observation, 'You can never learn what you already know.' That classic quotation might be considered the kernel of most management problems . . . it is found time and again that even a management in trouble will not be open-minded about the possibility of improvement."

He told of the president of one firm who would not listen to employing industrial engineers, because "I never saw one of them that was any good, and don't expect to now." It developed he had no experience, but simply had an opinion, and held to it.

"The irony of it was that the man was intelligent," said Symington. "Later he publicly corrected his previously held opinion."

He went on to say, "Industrial engineers are specialists. Why should they not get the job done?"

After this followed a series of well-thought-out discussions of administration, sales, operations, engineering, finance and other aspects of business management, all of which his audience received with approval. They showed that he knew what he was talking about.

Then he turned to the labor problem. Some of his paragraphs were pithy:

"A great French engineer once remarked, 'A worker doe.

not like to be ordered, but does like to work where order reigns.' "

"Management should mean the extension of order and simplicity right down to the worker on his machine."

"If this law [unemployment insurance] results in more employment, we are for it; because the great challenge to our present system is the problem of unemployment."

"Provided the basis is proper, we believe the closer management is to the employee, the less chance there will be for labor trouble; and the greater the opportunity for getting the production job done."

"The American worker is a sportsman. Give him a fair manager, who knows the game, show him the rules and the reasons, and he'll do his best to knock the ball over the fence."

"If . . . the Wagner act tends to promote understanding on the industrial ball club, we are 100 percent for it."

"A relationship of mutual respect is constructive. It tends to get relatively unimportant issues handled quickly and forgotten—and unimportant issues, allowed to continue, often become important."

"The Constitution states clearly who runs the show. The people have the power, so long as we stay a democracy. So why is it not wise to start educating them about the many problems of the American system?"

"We hear a lot of talk about dishonest people getting hold of unions. It is possible. They apparently even get hold of nations. They have been known to get hold of banks; and of great industries. Generally they get caught."

"We have been raised as masters of our government, not its servants. Today this same question points to our industrial life. Are we to become servants of our machines; or masters of them? Well, we made them. Therefore it is surely up to us to keep them running properly."

It is not of record whether the Society for the Advancement of Management loudly applauded this speech. But it is of record that his optimistic view of the new labor laws, and his recommendations concerning them are now generally accepted practice.

From that day, Stuart Symington was closely watched by American industry.

5

There was another phase of his policy that is worth mentioning. St. Louis is a border city with a mingling of northern and southern customs and feelings. When Symington arrived in 1938, it was ahead of most southern cities in racial attitudes, but well behind most northern cities. Except in public transportation there was a pattern of segregation. Job, educational, and other opportunities were depressingly limited. Few Negroes were in white collar, professional and skilled occupations, and few held elective public offices.

The change in which Symington was a leading factor, is described by George L-P Weaver, a highly intelligent and educated Negro, who is now assistant vice president of the I.U.E., and was an assistant of Symington's in some of his government work. Weaver saw what the St. Louis situation was, with interest, and his observations are as follows:

"Under the management of Symington and with support of the union, the Negro worker made tremendous advances at Emerson. Percentagewise, few other St. Louis industrial plants doing war work hired more Negroes, and at no other plant were conditions for and attitudes toward the Negro better. In the early years of Symington's direction of the company he drew upon the advice and counsel of a group of Negroes in the plant. They helped the union and management in the touchy problems of race, and in improving the process of integrating Negroes into production jobs. Therefore, while many other plants continued to assign Negroes to menial and unskilled labor tasks, Emerson instituted a policy of upgrading on merit and seniority to skilled and semiskilled jobs. One Negro was advanced to a supervisory job, unusual in those days, and others to semisupervisory jobs.

"Integration in and out of the plant was advanced. Segregation in the company's cafeteria was abolished. A joint social and recreational committee was set up, and Negroes attended parties and picnics sponsored by the company. They also participated fully in the profit-sharing plan and on an equal footing received the company's service awards. The morale of both white and Negro employees was high.

"The conservatives in the community who had regarded Symington as a dangerous upstart with radical ideas began considering him as a forward-looking executive, when success and prosperity came to Emerson. Peaceful labor and race relations were obviously a very important part of the reason.

"As in many other cities of the country, the war boom which opened in the 1940s increased racial frictions and tensions in St. Louis. The basic cause was competition for homes and jobs in the defense production effort. Within a few years the Negro population increased an estimated 40 per cent and new whites were pouring in too. All were seeking well-paying war production jobs and dwellings to live in. The burgeoning Negro population was compelled to spill over into white districts.

"There was considerable tension in St. Louis during those years, but it never broke out into violence. The 1943 race riots in Detroit alarmed the country as well as St. Louis. In September of that year Mayor Aloys P. Kaufman completed appointment of an interracial committee of sixty-five members, twenty-four of whom were Negroes. Symington, recognized for his handling of the Emerson situation, was one of those named.

"The Race Relations Commission was given credit for highly effective work in abating discrimination, prejudice and misconceptions, and for promoting good will and better understanding. It was also commended for improving Negro housing conditions, health, sanitation, education and recreation.

"During his seven years at Emerson, Symington earned the reputation in St. Louis as a liberal and progressive business executive with a progressive view of labor and race problems which he had quietly implemented at his industrial plant without preachment and fanfare.

"His policies at Emerson, which resulted in racial advancements, were not accomplished with publicity. His subsequent career in Washington has followed this pattern. The record of his actions has always spoken louder than his words."

VIII

"A LOAD OF COAL"

1

Meantime the Symingtons continued to go their way, a charming and happy group, who soon made a warm circle of friends, were much sought after, and were delighted with their new home and city.

Symington took a willing and hearty part in community affairs, and any St. Louis business leaders who had their fingers crossed on him soon uncrossed them. He was invited to join one of the better country clubs, was elected to the board of directors of the Chamber of Commerce and was a member of its airport committee, became a director of a large bank, was chosen for the important Committee for Economic Development, and served in the Interracial Committee, as has been noted.

Mrs. Symington, a patrician if there is such a thing in this country, was so warm-hearted, friendly, and delightful that she made hosts of devoted friends. The boys, Stuart and Jim, were growing up and going to school.

Then came the war. With the invasion of Poland, September 1, 1939, the whole world abruptly and tragically changed.

As it became more and more evident that the United

States would inevitably be drawn into the conflict, the Nation began to gather itself, and prepare. It was not long before the defense program began to eat into the domestic economy, and Symington began to look for something in the defense line to which he could convert his plant.

The airplane was proving itself a decisive factor in the war overseas, and the European battles, especially Dunkirk, had proved that gun turrets, if perfected sufficiently, would become a tremendously important adjunct of bomber armament.

The French had worked on developing an airplane turret, and failed. There was some work on development going on among American aircraft companies. But the British had led the world, and they placed their faith in turrets.

Symington, always interested in the air, went to Washington to see if he could make turrets for the United States. At first he was somewhat coolly received. But he kept at it. Eventually he met William S. Knudsen, head of the OPM.

The meeting was decisive. Knudsen believed in Symington after he talked to him, and officials of OPM flew back to St. Louis with Symington, examined his plant, and recommended vast enlargements and changes. His activities in the next few days were tremendous.

Thursday he flew to Washington to draw up a rough contract; Friday he went by air to New York and Buffalo to get some engineers who had turret experience at Bell, Curtiss-Wright, and elsewhere; Saturday he was in Detroit, discussing his proposed new plant with industrial engineers; Sunday, back in St. Louis, he led a group of architects over the rough ground next to his hermetics motor plant, where later the government spent $15,000,000 for a turret plant.

Monday he called a meeting of the board of Emerson and presented his proposal. According to one story, after a moment's silence one of the directors asked, "What in the hell is a turret?" But the project was approved even though they knew very little about it. They had faith in Symington.

Tuesday, Symington and his turret man flew back to Washington, where they were sworn in as special observers for OPM which qualified them for diplomatic passports, and on Wednesday, seven days after he began this frenetic series of moves, he left New York in a plane for England, to see British turrets firsthand and learn what he could about making them.

2

The Germans were conducting one of their blitz campaigns against Britain when Symington arrived, but that did not bother him or interfere with the thoroughness and rapidity of his observation. The British were cooperative—they wanted turrets too—and his extremely quick and retentive intelligence absorbed information like a blotter.

When he flew back to the United States and began getting Emerson in order to take on the big job, he had formed some original opinions. It had been planned at first to build standard British turrets for American planes; but Symington saw some flaws in the British design.

For one thing, the British, who bombed chiefly at night, insisted on .30 caliber guns, because the .50 calibers had a tendency to blind the gunners by their flash in the darkness. The United States, on the other hand, with the new theory of precision daylight bombing, stuck to the larger caliber.

For another thing, as he puts it, "The British turret was too small. It cramped the men. When a man gets cramped he gets cold, and when he gets cold he has fear, and when he is fearful he is no good as a fighter."

Symington's new turret, designed at Emerson in its own research laboratory, was adopted by the Army Air Force. Originally intended as a tail turret for the B-24 Liberator, it was soon shifted to the nose when its qualities became evident. Then other types of turrets were added to the list.

Emerson boomed and mushroomed. Where it had employed a few hundred men when Symington took over, it was now employing more than 11,000. He used the personnel department to keep the union leaders fully informed on the progress of the war and the needs for the help of every man. Morale was extremely high. Emerson, though not the largest plant in the city, led St. Louis in industrial contributions to the war chest drive, and donated the most blood to the Red Cross. When the first Emerson-designed turret was completed, Emerson employees bought it and gave it to the army, and more than ninety-five per cent of them participated.

Meantime production went up and up, the theoretical "potential" was exceeded over and over again. Where Emerson's peacetime peak had been $5,500,000, it climbed toward $100,000,000 a year.

Once again Stuart Symington had wrought the impossible.

3

One of the inevitable corollaries of being a large contractor for government materiel is that there will be government investigations. Emerson had received an "E" for its superior effort from both the Army and Navy, but a House committee visited it to investigate production methods, and then Senator Harry S. Truman, who was making his great reputation as a thorough and incorruptible head of the special Senate committee investigating the national defense program, arrived in St. Louis.

He went into matters thoroughly, received a full, honest, and complete report from Symington, and not only gave Emerson a clean bill of health, but was deeply impressed by the company's head.

Truman snapped, "It isn't you who ought to be investigated. It's the people who wanted you to be investigated."

He did not forget Stuart Symington, and as a result events were once again to change completely Symington's life.

With December 11, 1941, the United States was plunged into the war. Both Symington sons enlisted as soon as they became seventeen, Stuart in the Army and Jim in the Marines.

In that period of dire peril to the country, Symington worked so hard that it seriously imperiled his health, as will be seen. But Emerson kept turning out turrets and other war material in ever-increasing flow, as he stood at the throttle of the company.

On April 12, 1945, when the United States and its allies at last were on the march to victory, the world was stunned by the news of the death of President Franklin Delano Roosevelt.

Harry Truman, who had been elected Vice President as Roosevelt's running mate the previous fall, was at once sworn into office. He pledged himself to carry out the domestic and foreign policies of his great predecessor.

Followed historic months, as the war crashed to its close.

On May 8, President Truman announced to the Nation the final defeat of Germany.

On the night of August 14, he sent the whole United States into a vast jubilation by announcing the end of the global conflict with the surrender of Japan.

The close of the vast war posed new national problems. One of the most perplexing of these was the matter of disposal of surplus war materials of which nearly 13 billion dollars' worth of aircraft, industrial plants, machines, ships, raw materials, consumers' goods, and property of all kinds were on hand.

In June of 1945, after Germany's defeat, but before Japan's surrender, Symington received a call to Washington, to confer with the President. He was ushered into the President's office in the White House, and saw Mr. Truman smiling at him. He did not know what was in store for him, or how well the President thought of him, and the Chief Executive's first words were not reassuring.

"Stuart," he said, "I'm going to drop a load of coal on you."

"Sir—what do you mean?" Symington asked.

"I want you to become Chairman of the Surplus Property Board."

Dazed, Symington asked for time to consider. It was granted.

His friends, some of them, were aghast at the news. "Don't even think of such a thing!" they urged. "It's a graveyard. Think of what happened to the War Surplus Commission after World War I. Half of the people connected with it went to jail! It's so complicated and there are so many factors pulling this way and that, of which the worst is human greed, that you're bound to get into a jam no matter how hard you try."

At last he sought out his best friend and advisor, Senator Wadsworth, his father-in-law, who was now serving as a Representative in Congress, but still was called "Senator" by everyone.

"What shall I do?" Symington asked.

"The President of the United States has called upon you

to perform a difficult task for your country," said Senator Wadsworth gravely. "As an American you should be proud of it, and it is your duty to accept it and do your best with it."

"But I know nothing of politics. What about the pitfalls and blind alleys they talk about?"

The Senator smiled. "Son," he said, "I know you pretty well. Call them as you see them, and you'll get into no trouble."

Symington says that it was one of the greatest votes of confidence, coming from the source it did, that he received in his whole life.

With that to give him reassurance he called on the President again and said he was willing to accept the appointment. But first there was the little matter of confirmation.

It was at this point that the parking meter company, in which Symington was briefly interested back in early 1937, entered into the picture again. He had sold those interests when he took over the Emerson plant.

In 1942, while he was laboring at the limit of his strength on the war production at Emerson, he was waited upon by some gentlemen from the Department of Justice. They informed him that an automobile parking meter company, of which he had been president, had gotten into a little antitrust trouble with the government. Could he throw any light on the matter?

Symington at once agreed to turn over all his correspondence and papers regarding that brief episode of business as far as he was concerned. With the help of the information in his files, the Department of Justice convicted several parking meter companies or officials of violating federal antitrust laws.

When Symington was proposed for the Surplus Property Board, a newspaper columnist, digging into the files, brought

up the story that Symington was involved in antitrust transactions. Senator Joseph O'Mahoney, of Wyoming, chairman
of the committee which investigated the record of the man
the President wanted for the job, questioned him severely
about the parking meter matter.

Respectfully, Symington told the committee that he had
sold out all interests he had in the company when he went to
St. Louis and made available to the government any information he had bearing on it.

"You're not a defendant in this case?" roared O'Mahoney.

"No, sir," said Symington.

"You are aware," O'Mahoney continued, "that the objective of the law of Congress is that the surplus property
should be disposed of in such a manner as to encourage free
and independent enterprise and discourage monopolistic ac-
quisition of properties?"

"Yes, sir," said Symington, and added that he had always
fought monopolies.

"It would not be your inclination then," roared the Senator, "to deal leniently with applicants who might wish to use
this property for fastening monopolistic control upon any part
of the trade or commerce of the United States?"

"No, sir," said Symington.

He was released after this grilling. It had been a pretty
rough session, or so he thought, and he felt that Senator
O'Mahoney was hostile to him and would block his appointment. He sought out his father-in-law, and told him he was
sure his appointment would be blocked.

Senator Wadsworth, mellow with his years of experience,
calmed him down.

"Let's see what really is happening," he said. "I'll call
O'Mahoney. You can listen on my secretary's extension."

He called Senator O'Mahoney's office, and got him on the line. "Joe," he said, "how's this thing coming out about my son-in-law?"

"Why, Jim, it's in the bag," answered O'Mahoney, with all the cordiality in the world. "There's no question about the confirmation. Everybody's for him."

It was Symington's first experience with the sound and fury that sometimes makes politics appear other than what it is.

The Senate confirmed him to the post without one single dissenting vote, thus setting a sort of precedent, for it confirmed five more appointments of Stuart Symington with the same single-mindedness in the years to come.

4

Symington's first act, on receiving the appointment, was to sever his connections with all private business, including Emerson Electric, and sell all his holdings. He took a considerable financial loss by doing this, since he insisted on selling at once, although the stocks were rising rapidly on the market, because he did not want anyone ever to say that he had favored any concern in which he had an interest. Yet the sale of his Emerson stock, because of the enormous increase of its value due to his efforts during the war years and before, made him wealthy. Not, perhaps, wealthy in the sense that a Texas oil millionaire considers wealth, but well-to-do enough so he felt he could devote himself to the work of a public servant, without jeopardizing the future of his family. All of the money he received for his securities was placed in trusts.

But he quickly found that the Surplus Property Board was a clumsy organization, slow moving and indecisive because it had on it three men who frequently did not agree. This was contrary to every business tenet he knew.

With the surrender of Japan in August, the agency was reorganized on Symington's recommendation to the President, and on September 27, 1945, he was sworn in as sole Administrator of the new Surplus Property Administration.

He had just entered into the largest and trickiest merchandising enterprise in the world, and he was solely responsible for it.

At first he left Mrs. Symington in St. Louis, because he did not expect the job to be a long one. But before long he sent for her, and they took an apartment in the Shoreham Hotel. The job, it appeared, would be longer than he expected.

Before he was through, with a series of appointments every one of which was exacting, six and one-half years had passed.

IX

THE WAY OF A PUBLIC SERVANT

1

From the beginning of his administration of the Surplus Property Administration, Symington made himself a name for honor and integrity, and the ability to get along with people and get things done.

Very early his staff discovered that they had a new boss who believed in hard work and efficiency. It is recorded that Symington never spared himself, and if necessary he did not spare his staff. They worked late if that was required to get the work done, and the boss worked right with them.

One morning, early in his administration, he came into his office as usual at eight thirty, and pressed a buzzer to summon one of his assistants. There was no answer. Symington pressed another button. Still no answer.

Now very much interested, he pressed all the buttons on the intercom box at once. Only one member of his staff responded.

"Tell the others that there will be a staff meeting," Symington said, and named the hour.

The aide left and passed along the information.

When, at the hour named, the whole staff was assembled,

Symington made them a very brief, very pointed little speech.

"Gentlemen," he said, "let's get this straight. In this office, we arrive at eight-thirty because that is official regulations. And we stay late when necessary because we love our work. That's all."

Symington did love his work. He loves work of any kind, always enjoys anything into which he has to put intensive effort.

There were, of course, the usual "under the table" offers for concessions, made by venal persons or interests who could not believe that anyone else was not as easily corrupted as themselves.

One instance in point was when a man with a very well-known name—his brother was a famous star in the entertainment world—came to Symington's office, and tried to gain possession of the available supplies of silk without going through the usual details of inspection, appraisal, and competitive bidding. Symington bluntly refused.

The man laid on the desk a cashier's check for half a million dollars.

"Pick that up," said Symington.

The man made no move.

"If you don't pick it up, I'll tear it up into little pieces and throw it out of the window!" said Symington.

At that the man hastily picked up the cashier's check and departed.

The silk later was properly disposed of through the correct channels. It did not take very long for the word to get out, through various grapevines, that the new administrator could not be bought, coerced, or influenced.

Soon after he took over the office of the Surplus Property Administration, he made good on his promise that he would be a foe to monopoly. The Aluminum Corporation of America was in the market to take over all the huge government-built aluminum plants for wartime production, urging as a strong point that they owned patents necessary to the operation of those plants.

But a court ruling recently had held that Alcoa was a monopoly, at least for the present time. With that ruling before him Symington told the corporation that he could not sell those plants to it.

A high official of Alcoa paid him a visit and expressed sincere concern over the ruling and worry that the firm was getting a black eye in the public mind.

"You should be worried," said Symington. "Your name is becoming synonymous with monopoly."

The Alcoa official said his company wished very much to dispel that impression, and Symington had high hopes that he could make a successful negotiation with it.

To his surprise, Alcoa instead made charges against him, to the effect that he was "forcing a government subsidy plan on private industry," in a printed 45-page letter which was placed on the desk of every Senator and Congressman, and issued to the newspapers, the following week.

Symington was up in arms at such a personal attack on himself and his administration. He summoned his staff, and began to dig into the facts, to refute Alcoa's charges and claims. Together they came up with some interesting data. For instance, Alcoa had stated that its technical advances had materially reduced the price of aluminum. Symington and his aides showed that where aluminum was 16½ cents a pound in 1911, it was 15 cents a pound in 1946, and at times in the interim had been as high as 38 cents. A cent and a half was not much of a reduction for thirty-five years of "technical advances."

With this material he went right back at Alcoa in a 50-page report, sent to the same desks that the Alcoa letter had gone. There were some acrimonious exchanges, but the upshot was that the officials of Alcoa agreed to a conference in the office of Attorney General Tom Clark.

It was, as one account of the affair said, "a historic poker game with nearly a billion dollars at stake, and Symington played his cards like a suave Dangerous Dan McGrew." In the room were Attorney General Tom Clark and some of his staff; Wendell Berge, of the Justice Department's antitrust division; the Alcoa contingent headed by the executive vice president, I. W. Wilson, known as "Chief," Arthur V. Davis, chairman of the board, and a battery of the smartest lawyers that could be gathered; and Symington with his aides, Hugh Cox, Irv Lipkowitz, and Sam Moment.

Symington's hole card was the fact that the court had ruled Alcoa a monopoly, but had postponed any court action to break it up until the Surplus Property Administration acted. Alcoa's hole card was the fact that it owned patents for extracting aluminum from bauxite ore, and the government had to have them before any other firms could take over the war plants in question.

During the long conference Symington did not once waver, and it became increasingly evident as the day wore on that if Alcoa did not come to an agreement of some sort, it would certainly face the courts on the monopoly basis. When the meeting broke up at last, Alcoa agreed to present a new proposition within twenty-four hours.

It did so. Chief Wilson went to Symington's office next day with a new bid. Alcoa, he said, would release its patents to the government's Reconstruction Finance Corporation, on a fee basis.

And now the Symington charm came into play. He had been mad when Alcoa made its attack on him, but the anger had passed, and he was all smiling persuasion.

"Chief," he said, "as long as you've come this far, why don't you go all the way and really get credit for doing a good thing? Give your government the patents for free."

Wilson got up. "We'll *never* satisfy you!" he exclaimed, and walked out.

But a little later he called up. "Stuart," he said, "I guess you're right."

The patents were made over. Without them, or even with them on a fee basis, competition of other firms with Alcoa would have been difficult if not impossible.

The aluminum war plants were disposed of to strong companies that could successfully compete, in the years to follow.

There were hitches, of course; but in this period Symington won the name of being able to get along with Senators and Congressmen, because he treated them with respect and courtesy.

"Most Senators and Congressmen are honest and sincere," he says, "and they will listen if you tell them the truth as clearly as you can and as fully as they want to hear it."

He makes a fetish of getting facts, and getting them straight. On one occasion he was called to a hearing of the Senate Subcommittee on Surplus Property, when there was some real indignation over shabby treatment of veterans at a sale of surplus goods which had been advertised. A long line of ex-G.I.'s stood in the rain for hours and then could not buy any of the articles they wanted because there were only a few broken-down jeeps and trucks for sale.

Symington walked into the hearing, took his seat, and in a manner respectful, candid, and helpful, and with no attempt to gloss over the unpleasantness said:

"Gentlemen, I have had this disgraceful affair investigated thoroughly by Mr. Joseph Carroll, who, as you know, is one of the foremost investigators of the F.B.I. Here is Mr. Carroll's report."

He then analyzed the occurrence as a complete breakdown between the Smaller War Plants Corporation and the Department of Commerce, and outlined his plans for preventing a recurrence in the future. He received the hearty thanks of the Senators.

2

In this period of intensive effort, Symington did not have much time to play. A schedule that kept him long after hours forbade anything except an occasional golf game, evenings with his wife, a visit every two or three weeks to the White House for, as one man put it, "discussion and perhaps a little social pleasure." Harry Truman liked a *very* moderate little poker game for relaxation. And he liked friends to enjoy it with, men with whom he could laugh and joke and be at ease, and forget for a time his great responsibilities.

Mrs. Symington cooked breakfast for her husband, and dinner too, except for the occasional evenings out. Between times she made friends, and she is and always has been the kind of woman who makes and keeps devoted friendships with women as well as men, because she is charming, and understanding, and generous, and has none of that quality known as "cattiness" about her.

Bright spots were occasional visits to the home of Senator and Mrs. Wadsworth. The Hay-Adams house had been sold a number of years before and a hotel, called the Hay-Adams, erected on the site. The Wadsworth lived in Georgetown in an old house which had a long history.

Symington and the Senator, of course, differed heartily, openly, and sometimes heatedly on politics. The Senator was a Republican wheel-horse, his son-in-law an equally strong Democrat.

There is a record of a bit of correspondence, which shows that however they argued, the attachment between them was very strong. After a particularly violent argument in the Georgetown house, Symington sent his father-in-law a very penitent and affectionate note of apology. Here is what the Senator answered:

Dear Stuart:

Thanks for your good letter of January 17. By no means do you owe me an apology. If there is any guilt I should be charged with 60% of it. There isn't any guilt. The truth is you and I are born argufiers. I've known that about myself a long time, and it has not dismayed me one little bit to know that you possess the same talent.

I note from long experience the contest seldom starts before 10 p.m. . . . no time limit is set. Each contestant talks a little louder as time passes and a very important technique . . . is preventing your opponent ever finishing a sentence . . . It is much more important to be emphatic than logical . . .

This is what happened to us the other night and there is no use planning not to argue about it, for, like a spark in a powder barrel, a trifling observation may set it off. What you and I really need is the continued presence of a wife or a mother-in-law.

That twinkling note was a reiteration, in a different way, of Senator Wadsworth's statement made long before, "Young Symington is the kind of a man who looks you straight in the eye."

As to Symington during those days, one observer said of him:

"His social behavior is as effortless as his golf swing, and as effective; he has . . . engaging personal charm. Together with, and beyond this, he has style. If he lounges, walks, tells a story . . . or testifies before a committee, the action carries a certain innate air of distinction, as if this were, indeed, the right thing to do just then, and his the right way to do it."

A few months of continuous effort, and the big job was done. Without a hint of corruption or inefficiency or scandal, Symington had disposed of billions of dollars' worth of government property, ranging from vast manufacturing plants to safety pins and toothpicks, and on the best obtainable terms for the government. With Mrs. Symington he prepared to return to St. Louis.

But there was to be no rest. Another call came from the White House. The War Department was undergoing a reorganization, and the President wanted him to be Assistant Secretary of War for Air.

Harry Truman had a reason. Since the Spanish-American War, a plan to unify the armed forces for greater military cooperation and efficiency in a single Department of Defense had been discussed, and now a law was being proposed to put this reform into operation. The Navy, which considered Truman "an Army man" and feared it would be subordinated to the sister service, dissented, and it had been doing such a brilliant job of publicity and public relations that it appeared that the proposal was seriously losing ground.

The President wanted his trouble shooter to check that trend if possible, and monitor the bill through Congress.

By temperament and experience Stuart Symington believes in air power. He had made turrets for warplanes at Emerson

Electric, he knew many of the officers in the flying service, he had done a not inconsiderable amount of flying himself—some of it under near-battle conditions in the European theater during the war—he saw great future potentialities for the air arm of the Nation's forces, and he took the job.

In the long Congressional maneuvering that followed, he was the spearhead, and this brought him into sometimes heated arguments with a good friend of his, James Forrestal, who had become Secretary of the Navy, and was actively opposed to the measure to place all three armed services under a single civilian secretary.

The differences between the two men on this subject did not, however, in any way mar their friendship, and they would play golf together, and amicably continue their debates on the links, when they had time for such relaxation.

3

It was during this period that Symington confronted the only serious health problem of his life—and beat it.

It really began during his days at Emerson Electric, when he was driving his plant to its greatest effort in order to get done the work it was commissioned to do for the conduct of the war.

"I was working very hard," he says. "I suppose I wasn't very smart, and whenever I woke up in the morning, I'd get up. If I woke up at 3 o'clock in the morning, I'd get up and go to work.

"Things were at a very high pitch, with the whole plant straining to its utmost to fill the demands from the Government, and increasing in size, and so on. I had a room in the plant—with a bed—and some nights I'd even sleep out there.

We were working around the clock, so I could always get food at the cafeteria.

"During that period I must have been building up a case of high blood pressure, but I didn't know it until I went to Washington.

"In 1945, after I took on the Surplus Property job, I began having headaches, and they got worse. At first I didn't pay any attention to them. Then, in March, 1946, I had a really terrible headache. It bothered me so that I went to a doctor.

"He examined me and said my blood pressure was too high. They put me on a diet, but it didn't do much good. Finally, I asked the doctor what to do about it, and he said I ought to take it easy. Take it easy? How could I?"

The doctor then told Symington of a relatively new operational technique called a sympathectomy; a rather severe operation in which the sympathetic nerves of the back are severed, reducing the tension that causes high blood pressure.

Symington did not "take it easy." And in spite of the diet things got very bad in the spring of 1947, after he had been working especially hard on his duties as Assistant Secretary of War for Air. At that time the headaches became frequent and almost unbearable.

"The point was," he says, "I either had to stop working, in the opinion of my doctor, or run the risk of high blood pressure breaking out into something. It can cause hemorrhages of the eyes, or in the kidneys, or you might have a stroke. I've always had the best of health, and I decided I would undergo the operation."

He was told that the operation was by no means guaranteed to be 100 per cent successful. About one-third of the patients on whom it was performed derived no help from it; another third got some relief; but there was the final third who were completely cured.

"The surgeon who perfected the technique of sympathectomy was in Boston, Dr. Reginald Smithwick," he says. "I went to Boston and talked to him. He gave me a very thorough examination, a series of tests over a period, and when he was through with the tests he said that he would rather operate on me than on anybody he ever had, because I reacted so well to the tests. The tests showed I would heal up properly and there was nothing organically wrong with me. Some people who have things organically wrong aren't much improved, but I had never had anything wrong with me.

"The operation itself is rather serious, although not actually dangerous to life. They do it on two sides, one side first and then the other side. This was the spring of 1947, and I underwent the operation. It was a complete success."

While he was convalescing, among many messages he received was one from his friend James Forrestal, saying jokingly, "Stay in the hospital a long time. It will keep you out of my hair."

But his period of convalescence was surprisingly short.

"You're supposed to be out of commission for six months," he says, "and I was playing golf in three months, and back at my desk not long after that. Dr. Smithwick once kiddingly told me that I was his prize example of success. I've never had a headache in my life since I had the operation, and I used to have bad ones every week. I have frequent physical examinations, and there is never a trace of high blood pressure. They say they don't do the operation any more because of miracle drugs they have discovered, but I'd rather have it. Since the day I had the operation I've done anything I wanted to, eaten everything I wanted, drunk anything I wished, no low-salt diet, nothing."

The cure was 100 per cent. As Clark Clifford says, "That sympathectomy cured him as completely as an appendectomy cures appendicitis."

He went back to work in good health and filled with his old energy and mental drive. And he accomplished something besides helping push through the National Security Act, which passed Congress and became a law when it was signed by the President on July 26, 1947.

The Air Force had long been trying to gain a separate identity under the over-all Department of Defense, and it was Symington, the Assistant Secretary of War for Air, who was one of the chief figures in gaining this status when the defense bill was finally passed.

In the reorganization the United States Air Force was established as an autonomous armed service on September 18, 1947. That same day, by well-earned right, Stuart Symington moved up to become the first Secretary of the Air Force in our history, under James Forrestal, the former Secretary of the Navy, who became the first Secretary of Defense in the new arrangement.

X

THE PRESIDENT'S TROUBLE SHOOTER

1

Symington made a great Secretary of the Air Force, fighting its battles and working for its objectives in the first years of its organization and establishment. He saw that merit was rewarded and enforced discipline.

In the earliest days, he challenged entrenched bureaucracy by dismissing a man who flagrantly ignored an order. The friends of the person fired, senior bureaucrats, went to war for him, said he could not be discharged because the civil service rules would not allow it, the man was to valuable by reason of his experience and service, a top civil servant was untouchable, and other reasons.

Symington did not hesitate. He went directly to the Civil Service Commission, and got an immediate ruling that insubordination was grounds for dismissal. Then he put it directly: either the bureaucrat went, or he would resign.

"I've never had a job of responsibility without the authority to go with it," he said.

He was upheld by the President. When that was settled, he called in the man he had discharged, had a serious little talk with him about duty and the necessity of following orders, received his apology, shook hands with him, and ordered him back on the job.

Symington had, and still has, a great love for the air service, and a complete belief that it is as yet our best defense if it came to war.

Very soon after he took his new office, he said that the United States needed not less than 630 heavy bombers, on widely scattered bases, to insure national safety. He was one of the architects of the Strategic Air Command, and believes that even now it is our one best protection, until the intercontinental ballistic missiles reach a greater stage of perfection and production.

With his usual energy and persuasiveness he worked for the objectives he believed necessary, and sometimes he trod on toes of important people. When he did so, he made haste to set things right in his cordial manner, trying to keep disagreement from growing into serious rupture of personal friendships, but he did not recede from his position.

He was in a spectacular fight for the B-36 superbomber, and won a showdown battle with the Navy. During this period, to his sorrow, he was engaged in a long period of disagreement over policies with his old and close friend, Forrestal. The Secretary of Defense wanted a "balanced force" of Army, Navy, and Air Force, and when the new economy drive slashed the appropriations for the defense branches, he thought they should take the cut equally among them.

With this Symington took strenuous issue. He was sincerely sure that the long-range bomber force, which could fly atomic weapons to faraway targets, was the best investment the United States could make in the defense line. It was not in his nature to play the game any other way, than to go directly to his superior who disagreed with him and ask if he might state his views openly to a Congressional committee. Forrestal, with his usual breadth of viewpoint, granted his lieutenant the permission to speak his mind freely.

The newspapers had a field day over the controversy in Congress, and some admirers of Forrestal criticized Symington for opposing his chief, charging that he had "oversold" the idea that "air power is peace power."

To this Symington's reply, sometime later, delivered with the dry Symington humor, was unanswerable:

"It would be a right interesting thing for us now, wouldn't it, if we didn't have the long-range bombers and the SAC?"

Forrestal himself did not hold any of the resentments some of the service heads seemed to feel against Symington because of his successful battle for the Air Force. The two of them continued, once a week with the old camaraderie, their golf games throughout the period when they were at loggerheads over the policies of the Department of Defense.

Events have proved that Symington was absolutely right in his fight for air power. His thinking is continuous and pervasive, and it ranges over countless factors of his problems. He does not make up his mind on an issue until he has considered every possible side of it, but when he does—as in the Air Force controversy—he is all out for it, and petty considerations mean nothing to him compared to the larger issues he is fighting for, in that instance greater protective power for his country.

It was during Symington's tenure of the office of Secretary of the Air Force that President Truman issued his executive order for the integration of races in the armed services.

Symington went to the White House and called on Truman.

"Mr. President," he said, "do you mean this order? Because if you do it's going to be enforced."

"I mean every word of it," said Truman.

"All right. It will be done," said Symington, and departed.

His first move was to call in all the Air Force generals who were of Southern family or background.

"Gentlemen," he said, "all of us are Southerners by birth or descent. Both my grandfathers fought for the Confederacy in the Civil War, and the one whose name I bear was in Pickett's Charge at Gettysburg, and surrendered with Lee at Appomattox. That makes us all start even in traditions and history.

"Now the President of the United States has issued an executive order for the integration of the races in the armed forces. I personally believe it is only right and just, and erases barriers that should not exist, and in the long run will be for the benefit of all the fighting forces. But even if I didn't agree with it as I do, the order of the Commander-in-Chief would be enforced to the letter in this branch of the service. I've called you here, because I want to know if any of you dissent. If you do, I would like you to say so now."

Not a single one of the Southern generals dissented. On the contrary, to a man they expressed complete willingness to aid in the step.

Symington next looked around for someone to carry out the new policy. James Carey, whom he had helped fight Communism in the International Electricians' Union, was active then as now in working for civil rights, and Symington asked his advice. As a result, George L-P. Weaver, a highly intelligent and very tolerant and understanding Negro, an official of the electricians' union, was loaned to him to give suggestions in policy making.

Wisely and yet firmly, Symington proceeded to lead the way in integrating the armed services by doing it first in the

Air Force, with smooth efficiency and a maintenance of high morale throughout.

He had made a brilliant record as Secretary of the Air Force, but when Forrestal was replaced as Secretary of Defense by Louis Johnson, and another economy wave sliced the Air Force down to forty-eight wings in the pre-Korea expense-cutting drive, he resigned.

He had won his major battles, and established the Air Force on a sound footing. He felt it was time for someone else, who better agreed with what he considered unsound economy, to take over.

2

President Truman knew of his feeling, and when Symington offered his resignation, there was another task awaiting him.

The National Security Resources Board, organized to mobilize America's resources in the event of war, lacked a chairman. It had, in fact, lacked a chairman for fifteen months, since the Senate refused to confirm Mon C. Wallgren of Washington, for the post. In the meantime the agency had become practically moribund. With the "cold war" at full tension, Truman wished to revive it and get it to moving. He asked Symington to take the chairmanship.

The Senate had refused to confirm Wallgren for the post, but there was no such dissension when Symington was proposed. As it had done four times before—when he was named for chairman of the War Surplus Board, administrator of the War Surplus Administration, Assistant Secretary of War for Air, and Secretary of the Air Force—it gave him unanimous approval. He took up his new duties April 10, 1950.

He found the NSRB in deplorable condition, in organization and in morale. It had been an orphan child so long that it hardly knew what it was there for.

The first thing was to inject life and *esprit de corps* in it. Symington called his staff together, and gave them a "fight talk" reminiscent of the sort football coaches are supposed to make to their assembled squads just before the opening whistle of the big game.

Then he began reorganizing, putting employees in places where they seemed to fit well, and bringing in outside personnel to fill vacancies. Under his leadership, the sagging agency came to life, and began to function. By the time the Korean War began, it was doing a good job.

The Korean War, which started June 25, 1950, made the NSRB suddenly an agency of tremendous strategic importance, and by that time Symington already had it in full gear, functioning like a well-oiled and well-geared machine.

In those days Robert Coughlan wrote of him:

> He is a great executive; by almost universal acknowledgment, one of the best in the Administration, and, for that matter, in the whole country. He has enthusiasm, intuition, persuasiveness, directness ("an instinct for the jugular" as one of his staff says) and the indefinable but important asset of personal charm . . . Beyond this he has integrity and sincerity and the taut, driving energy to carry through on anything he starts.

In his administration, Symington used voluntary controls as much as he could. But when it became necessary he cracked down on hoarders of certain materials, and sharply warned price-raisers that if voluntary means failed, price controls and rollbacks would be certain to follow.

He succeeded, not only in obtaining valuable quantities of essential raw materials from abroad and elsewhere, but, according to the findings of the Senate Armed Services Committee, by bargaining and maneuvering he saved the nation $500 million in the short period he directed the NSRB. His exhaustive report to the President at the time of his resignation in 1951 is considered today a classic on the materials-manpower subject.

When the Office of Defense Mobilization began to overlap the functions of the NSRB, Symington, who believes above all in efficiency and no duplication of work and other functions, resigned and recommended that the two agencies be consolidated into one.

3

For the sixth time President Truman called him to the White House, to talk with him about yet another troubleshooting job.

The Reconstruction Finance Corporation, through mismanagement and talk of "favoritism" and "influence," had fallen to a record low in public esteem, and was being subjected to a withering investigation by a Senate committee of which James Fulbright, Democrat, of Arkansas, was chairman.

Truman said, "Stuart, I want you to clean up the RFC for me."

"If you'll give me full authority, Mr. President," said Symington.

"You'll be the one-man boss," said Truman.

So for the sixth time Symington's name was sent to the Senate as a Presidential appointee, and for the sixth time it was confirmed without one dissenting vote, which in itself is something that may be a record in American government.

Symington studied the RFC, and found it was indeed in an

extremely bad state. There was, he concluded, only one way that the standing of the multimillion-dollar Government lending agency could be rehabilitated. That was to establish a register, where every person calling at the agency about a loan would have to sign his name and give details of his connection with the loan; and give full public information on every loan granted. This was the so-called Goldfish Bowl policy, which he instituted. On the other hand, loans turned down were not to be published, because, in his own words, "That would hurt a company, turned down by what, you might say, is the last resort."

One night he invited several friends, including Justice William O. Douglas of the Supreme Court, Paul Porter, Abe Fortas, and others to a dinner at the Chevy Chase Country Club. The subject he wanted to talk about was the RFC and he wanted their advice.

"This is a really horrible mess," he told them. "I've seen some bad ones, but this is the worst in my experience."

He described to them his intended policy, and then went on, "Look, I've got to get the best public relations man in town, or I can't stay over there, because that place is in real trouble, and I just can't do what has to be done without someone to explain some of the things I've got to do in the best possible light, and give fullest public information on the transactions of the agency."

They considered, and then, as he relates it:

"They said, 'We don't know who the best public relations man in town is, but we know who is the best one in the world is.'

"I said, 'That's a big statement. Who's that?'

"And they said, 'A guy named Jimmie Allen.' I found he was somewhere out on the Coast, and Abe Fortas said, 'You can't get him, I don't think, he's in some sort of business out there.'

"But I said I'd talk to him, and I called him up. He said, over long distance, 'Hello, Mr. Symington, how are you?' I said, 'I'd like to talk to you about something.' He said, 'By any chance you're not trying to get me back in that rat race in Washington, are you?'

"'Oh, no,' I said. 'That's the farthest thing from my thoughts.' So he laughed. We understood each other right away, and we talked awhile, and two weeks later he moved his furniture here and went to work at the RFC."

It sounds simple, that way. But the episode illustrates one of Symington's most pronounced assets—the ability to get superior men to work with him. He had done it over and over. Not only did he get Jimmie Allen, who was a key man in restoring to the RFC public confidence in the months that followed, but others of equal stature, such as:

Peter Bukowski, Chicago banker whom he made deputy administrator; Solis Horowitz, general counsel; Edward C. Welsh, economist; Spencer Shannon, critical materials expert; Don S. Burrows, controller; Ramsay Potts, national security problems; Dabney Penick, investments; and George L-P. Weaver. Some of these men had served with him on the Security Resources Board or in the Air Force. Others had caught his eye elsewhere. In other words, he took his own "team" with him into RFC.

He was proud of his staff. Describing them, in a speech before the National Bankers Association, he said:

"At the RFC we have been lucky. New additions include a young colonel with a superb combat record, once the outstanding scholar at his university; a successful partner in one of your great banking houses, willing to dig in and help; a brilliant prosecutor, recommended unconditionally by a great tax law professor at Harvard; an economist with an outstanding record in occupied Japan; a gifted and penetrating auditor; and the former head of the world's largest group of stores, now again serving his government."

It was while he was head of the RFC that Symington tangled with another giant adversary, the world-wide Tin Cartel.

Tin is a metal of which the United States produces nothing, although tin ores are smelted and processed in this country. The chief sources of the native metal today are Bolivia, Indonesia, and Malaya, with a small amount coming from Nigeria.

The Tin Cartel, one of the last of the old classic combinations of interests in separate countries to keep a product priced above competitive levels, saw a rich opportunity for aggrandizement in the necessities of the American Government. In August 1950, the price of tin was 72 cents a pound. By April 1952, it was up to $2 a pound.

Then Symington discovered that 30,000 tons of tin had simply disappeared from the world market. To him the cause of this "disappearance" was obvious. Speculators intended to hold it for soaring prices, and through his own sources of information he learned that the price aimed for was a staggering $4 a pound.

He acted decisively. At his order the United States simply stopped buying tin. Before taking the step, he got the Munitions Board to agree to release enough of the metal it had stockpiled, to take care of essential needs, on the promise to pay it back when tin was once more available.

The results were spectacular. The tin market simply collapsed. There were screams from all over the world. In Singapore, the *Straits Times*, in an angry editorial, branded the action as "Symingtonism." Said the *Washington Daily News* of this outcry:

> In Singapore they call it "Symingtonism."
> There may be worse words—but not if you're in the tin or rubber business.
> The bogeyman is Stuart Symington . . . the trouble with our RFC head, as Singapore sees it, is that he wants to hold down prices. He won't buy if the big producers of rubber and tin try any gouging.
> All of a sudden, this awful man—whose name was unknown to people there a year ago—has begun to haunt their waking hours.

In particular the State Department was concerned over furious complaints from Bolivia, which was hard hit by the collapse in the prices of tin. Representations were made to Symington.

He stuck to his guns, but agreed to send a fact-finding commission to Bolivia to discover just what was the effect of the falling tin market on the economy of that country, and to study the cost factors.

And here occurred an incident illustrating the manner in which he stands up for his men.

As one member of the commission, which was headed by Dr. Edward C. Welsh, he nominated George Weaver. Someone from the State Department raised a question: Bolivia had no Negroes, and would it be diplomatic to send one to them on the commission?

At that Symington "hit the ceiling," as one of his associates later recalled.

"George Weaver is an American citizen," he said, "and a very able one! If the RFC sends a commission to Bolivia,

George Weaver is not only going, but he is going as a senior member!"

Weaver went, and a better choice could not have been made. He did such valuable service both in fact-finding and diplomacy, that the President of Bolivia had his picture taken, arm in arm with him, both smiling with cordiality.

4

Jimmie Allen, now a topflight executive in one of the big aircraft companies of Los Angeles, has some vivid memories of the early days in the RFC.

"Shortly after Symington took over the old RFC," he recalls, "he brought all of the branch managers—some fifty or sixty of them—in for a two-day conference to spell out the new ground rules.

"Meeting all of these men for the first time in the RFC's big conference room, Symington asked that they come up one after another and introduce themselves. He greeted each one with a warm hand-shake, repeating each man's name.

"At the close of the conference, forty-eight hours later, he gave a dinner for the assembled managers at a Washington hotel. Getting up to speak on the dais, Symington faced a dozen round tables with five or six men at each. He said, 'I haven't had much time to get to know you, but let me see if I at least remember your names.' Then, starting at one end of the room, he went around each table calling each man by name until he had covered the whole room. It was a stunt— and yet it had the effect of endearing him to every one of the men present. They felt that a man who could do that could also pull the RFC out of its troubles.

"A friend asked Symington how he managed such a feat of

memory. He dismissed it, saying, 'Perhaps the ability to remember is in inverse proportion to intelligence.'

"But then, reminiscing, he recalled that in his early days
he had gone to work for a company whose head insisted that
all new employees take a memory course. The memory teacher
started the course by covering a blackboard with names.
Erasing what he had written, the instructor turned to the
class and asked, 'Can any of you remember any of the names
that were on the blackboard?' Symington meekly got up and
repeated every name. That broke up the memory course for
that company."

His memory is phenomenal, and so is his courage. When
he took over the RFC, he recognized that strong measures
had to be taken to erase the public image of the RFC as an
easy-going money lender, rather casual with the taxpayers'
funds. He began by inisisting that "the RFC should bristle
with integrity," a phrase he borrowed from Justice Oliver
Wendell Holmes.

Symington received a lot of kidding from his colleagues in
other branches of government over this phrase.

"Are you bristling today?" one agency head asked him.

Rather briskly, Symington replied, "I think the boss [Harry
Truman] would prefer bristles to mink in this administration."

He cleaned up the RFC and in the process he fired a good
many "political appointees" with "connections." One of these
was no less a person than Mrs. Donald Dawson, then the
wife of Truman's patronage advisor.

If the President disagreed with that particular dismissal,
he never mentioned it to Symington, who was doing a really
magnificent job rehabilitating the RFC.

In fact he retained Truman's respect and regard through all his administrations.

In reorganizing the RFC he was, as always, a stickler for sound and proper organization. It is his creed that there are three things a man needs to know to do his job: (1) To whom do I report? (2) Who reports to me? (3) What job am I expected to do?

Once Symington illustrated this by quoting a well-known steel executive who, when asked before a Congressional committee who reported to him in his steel company, replied, "My secretary, two airplane pilots, and the executive vice president." To Symington that represented organization, the way a company should be run.

One of the vexing problems before the RFC was the rubber program. During the war the RFC had built synthetic rubber plants to supply the lack of natural rubber, and the whole synthetic rubber program was carried over in the RFC with many delicate questions to adjudicate where free enterprise and Government administration crossed.

Symington's method of handling was typical of his approach to large issues. He called in some of the most important men in the rubber industry, including the following:

John L. Collyer, president of Goodrich; H. S. Firestone, chairman of Firestone; A. L. Freedlander, president of Dayton; Frank D. Hendrickson, president American Hard Rubber; H. E. Humphreys, president U.S. Rubber; P. W. Litchfield, chairman of Goodyear; Everett Morss, president of Simplex Wire; Thomas Robins, Jr., president of Hewitt-Robins; and J. Penfield Seiberling, president of Seiberling.

These he formed into a Rubber Advisory Committee. Assembling them at Washington, he gave them a beautiful luncheon, and when he rose to address them he did not lecture them. Instead, he said in substance, "Gentlemen, this is your Government, and these are your problems. I've brought you here to ask you for your counsel. Please think over these matters which will be brought up and have been brought up, and tell me what to do."

His frankness and respect for the leaders of their field won them. He did not turn his administration over to them, but he did get the rubber industry to thinking for the Government. In other words, he never forgot that he was doing a job for the RFC, but in doing it he reached far better results through a sympathetic understanding on the part of the industry with which he was dealing.

He worked for American business, too. Before the House Committee on Appropriations, he pleaded:

"We are spending millions and billions to rehabilitate private enterprise in foreign nations," he said. "It is wrong for us to spend a few millions to rehabilitate private enterprise in our own?"

By the end of 1951 he had completed the task of putting the RFC back on its feet both in internal efficiency and integrity, and in public estimation, and all without a breath of scandal or hint of favoritism or special privilege extended to anyone.

He offered his resignation, and it was accepted effective January 15, 1952, by President Truman in a letter which said in part:

> Dear Stu: It is difficult to sever official bonds formed during my first months in the White House . . . With utmost reluctance, therefore, I accept the resignation . . .
>
> Yours has been not only a long but a varied service . . . Six full years of arduous effort in five posts of high responsibility . . . had given you exceptional training for the RFC. Besides so

rich and diverse a background of experience, you brought to that office last May courage, vision, integrity, sound judgment and a firm determination to serve the national interest. Promptly and wholeheartedly you assumed the task of building up public confidence in that Agency. It is a great satisfaction to me to have your assurance that the Agency is in good shape and functioning properly.

So I say to you: well done, and heartily reciprocate your warm personal sentiments. You have my best wishes for long years of health and happiness.

Sincerely yours, Harry S. Truman.

The Senate gave a warm recognition of his services in speeches by Senators McKellar and McClellan from the Democratic side, and Senator Knowland from the Republican side. The House also made a special occasion to pay tribute to Symington's distinguished contributions to the Government. In summing it up Wright Patman said:

"Even those who have quarreled over some of his actions have never doubted his sincerity, his honesty or his ability. The Nation can ill afford to lose the services of such a fine public servant during the present emergency. 'Stu' Symington deserves a rest, but I am hopeful that at some time in the future he will again take up the burden of public service which he has carried so ably in the past."

Congress Patman was in a sense a prophet, although Symington did not take that "rest." Instead, he went back to his home in Missouri to tackle another "impossible" task— and decisively defeat in his historic first race for the Senate two "old pro" politicians with powerful vote-getting machines behind them.

5

One of Stuart Symington's deep sadnesses, and even more so Mrs. Symington's, was the death of Senator Wadsworth, June 21, 1952. That great and wise man, Symington's father-in-law, political opponent, sage advisor, and beloved friend, had retired from active political life and his Congressional seat, making the announcement of his intention in May 1950, but serving out his term to January 2, 1951.

Though a Republican he loyally supported the Democratic administration in the Korean War national emergency. When, after his retirement from Congress, the Republican Party tried to capitalize on the President's dismissal of General Douglas MacArthur, he expressed his opinion of such tactics in a letter:

> What a row over MacArthur! That proposal to have him address Congress is atrocious. Suppose George Patton had done it! Or any Army or Navy officer rebuked by the Commander-in-Chief. Cheap politics!

This from a rock-bound Republican who was first of all an American above politics.

Senator Wadsworth's thirty-six years in the two houses of Congress had been distinguished by many notable acts, but his interest and continual sponsorship of a high defense program was one of its most important contributions. Even after his departure from Congress he had been induced by the President to serve on the National Security Training Commission, and received a sincere letter of gratitude from Harry Truman for his services and self-sacrifice.

He was ill even then, and his death in a Washington hospital was mourned by his friends of both parties throughout the Nation.

In some things Wadsworth and Symington differed strongly. But in one matter they were in wholehearted and sincere agreement. The old Senator all his long career in public service had been a sponsor and ardent advocate of a strong and alert defense establishment for his Nation.

To this the new Senator also had pledged his whole strength. When he first stepped on the floor of the Senate, Stuart Symington was identified in the minds of all with the issues surrounding national defense.

XI

A FRESHMAN SENATOR

1

When a "freshman" Senator takes his seat in that august body, he is "at the bottom of the table," as the saying is, when committee appointments are made, since seniority plays a powerful part in the composition of committees, particularly important ones.

Yet Senator Symington, though new as a member, was far from new to the Senate as a person. Unlike most freshman Senators, he knew his way around Washington, had an acquaintance with most of the important men in it, except for some of the new Eisenhower appointees, and was not long in getting acquainted with them and making friends of most of them.

"When you meet people and get to know them, it's not hard to make friends," is a saying of his.

His six and a half years of service in executive government positions, with frequent meetings with Senate committees of various kinds, together with his unblemished record as an exceptional administrator, had erected a high respect and regard for him. As a result he received immediate attention, and few freshman Senators have risen more rapidly.

His first committee appointment was the one he most
desired: to the important Armed Services Committee, which
handles legislation dealing with national security and military
preparedness. In announcing this appointment, Senator
Lyndon Johnson of Texas made a special point of stressing his
high qualifications through his experience as Secretary of the
Air Force and Chairman of the National Security Resources
Board.

He also received appointment to another big committee in
which he was by nature interested, and for which he was by
ability and experience qualified: the Government Operations
Committee, which keeps an eye on the operations of the
Government with a view to greater efficiency.

He and Mrs. Symington took up residence in the Georgetown house, which had been the home of Senator Wadsworth,
and belonged to Mrs. Symington's mother. There they lived
very simply.

The junior Senator from Missouri entered into his new
duties with the same well-directed energy that made a success
of his previous important Government jobs. Already, before
he had been in office much more than a year, his personality
and insight had made such an impression that the St. Louis
Globe-Democrat stated, "The prestige of Missouri in the
Senate rose to its highest in 30 years."

He was tireless in behalf of his home state, and his record
of accomplishments for Missouri is notable. It ranges from
flood control and industrial development assistance, to drought
and tornado disaster relief, and countless small, personal
services for his constituents. And he was always for the people
who lack what is known as "influence."

"They get pushed around," he says. "Take myself as an

example. In 1952 I knew I needed another phone, because Evie was complaining about the amount of phone time I was using at the house. So I called up the phone company. I said, 'I'd like another phone.' And the girl said, 'We haven't got any more phones.' And I said, 'Well, give me the other company, please—the other phone company.' She said, 'Mister, are you trying to be funny?' I said, 'No, I'm not trying to be funny. I want a phone, and I've got the money to pay for it, and I'd like to have the phone.' She said, 'I told you we didn't have any more phones.'

"Well, at that I asked for the supervisor, and she put the supervisor on. I went through the whole rigmarole again, and finally I said, 'Listen, please. Will you tell whoever you work for that my name is Stuart Symington, and I'm going to run for the United States Senate, and I can't do it without another phone? I want another phone.' And then I gave her my telephone number.

"In about an hour a call came from the vice president of the phone company. He said, 'We'll have a phone in your house within an hour.'

"Now that was just a matter of persistence, and using whatever influence I had. It's the kind of thing that goes on all over America all the time. Because I happened to be running for an important office the phone company was in a hurry to oblige me with a phone.

"But suppose now that I was Joe Doaks, and business had gotten so good in my hot-dog stand or little garage that I couldn't possibly handle it with one phone. Would I get one in a hurry? No, I'd have to stand in line, hat in hand, and maybe wait for weeks or months, and maybe never get it. That's what I mean about people being pushed around."

2

There was one instance when Symington really got mad over that sort of "pushing around."

Congressman Charley Brown, the highly personable and intelligent young Representative from the southwest Missouri district, which never sent a Democrat to Congress since the Civil War, before he ran and was elected, tells the story best:

"We had a bridge problem in southwest Missouri when I was running for my first term. The Table Rock dam had been built to impound the waters of the White river, and the backwaters of the reservoir were inundating a steel bridge across that stream. The bridge had been built by the people of two small towns, Viola and Shell Knob, which were on opposite sides of the river, and they had bonded themselves to erect it so that they all could attend the same church and send their children to the same school.

"To those people in the little twin villages, the loss of 'their bridge' meant that the Viola church members would have to drop out of the church, because they couldn't drive thirty-five to forty miles around to another bridge every Sunday, and they would lose their community center, the little school house.

"Some of them came to me. Well, I frankly didn't expect to get elected—no Democrat had in that district since the Year One, almost. So I asked the people to talk to Senator Symington who was touring Missouri at the time. They sent a delegation to wait on him at Cassville and tell him about losing 'their bridge.'

"Symington listened attentively and said, 'I'll look into it.' He asked for a report from the Corps of Engineers about the Shell Knob bridge.

"The Corps of Engineers passed the buck to the Missouri State Highway Commission. The Highway Commission said that all the bridge relocations in the Table Rock area had been approved, the contracts signed, and the matter was closed.

"That was when Symington got mad. He said, 'It isn't closed. You're inundating a bridge that these people paid for themselves. You're not paying them for it. You're not replacing it. You're pushing them around, because they're so few in number, and you're not going to get away with it.'

"By this time it was January 1957, and Congress had convened. I had been elected to Congress, and Symington and I went to the Corps of Engineers, then we went to the Chairman of the Appropriations Committee, then back to the Corps, then to the Governor of Missouri, and back to the Missouri State Highway Commission.

"You would have thought that the Shell Knob bridge was America's answer to the Sputnik, Symington was so determinde that the bureaucrats weren't going to mistreat those people like that.

"Well, we got the bridge replaced. The people of the Viola-Shell Knob community in Missouri still have their church and their joint community activities in the schoolhouse, have their direct mail service and a shorter distance to market their milk."

3

But his interest and care for the business of his state did not dim or obscure his attention and activities for the national welfare. He had once been a close friend and admirer of Dwight D. Eisenhower, but as he watched the new President's policy, or rather lack of policy, he began to lose his esteem.

Especially did this become true when he found himself almost a "lone voice in the wilderness" as he protested against and fought the lackadaisical attitude of the Administration toward what he passionately considered the prime necessity of the country, that it be strong militarily.

A Missouri paper, the *Warsaw Enterprise*, gave an interesting comparison and appraisal in this matter:

> During the fateful years between World War I and II there was one major dissenting voice as the world's Democracies junked their navies and disbanded their armies.
>
> The voice was Winston Churchill's. His position was not a popular one in a world that desperately wanted peace at any price—even, as it turned out, at the price of peace.
>
> The obvious rise of Naziism vindicated Churchill's stand.
>
> In the vastly more critical period following World War II the Free World once again followed "economy" to blind it to the armaments advances being made by a tyranny which masquerades as a revolution.
>
> Democracy seems to produce, in such times, at least one far-seeing man who'll decry the clipping of Samson's locks—in a modern sense, the research laboratories as well as the armed services.
>
> America brought forth this man and Missouri voters sent him to the U.S. Senate where his voice cried out against arms and research slashes.
>
> Sen. Stuart Symington's stand, like Churchill's, was not popular. But he did not sway before the tide of economy which swept through Congress. He put the power of his background and logic behind President Eisenhower when members of the President's own party were being swept along in the economy wave. And he was left to battle almost alone when the President himself wavered on how much money was needed to keep this Nation mighty.
>
> But stick it out he did—and, at a critical time, the enemy sent aloft proof that the Senator was correct. The huge Sput-

niks proved that what the Senator had called the Eisenhower policy of "drift and dream" had allowed the Reds to snatch military superiority—even in the technical fields.

The Senator has proved he knows what he is talking about. The Nation, increasingly, is leaning on his words.

That editorial was written after the launchings of the Russian Sputniks, but it accurately evaluates the long and sometimes lonely battle Symington has carried on.

He was, during his Secretary of the Air Force days, the first to foretell accurately the rise of Soviet military power, and as a Senator was a leading figure in debates, not only on the Senate floor, but in committee, on questions of the national defense over which he was so greatly concerned.

4

But national defense was by no means his only interest. One of the most interesting things to watch, after his first election to the Senate, was the manner in which he dug into and mastered the complexities surrounding the problem of agriculture.

Before he ran, and even during his first campaign, he could only tell the people that he would do for agriculture everything that was in his power. After he was elected he implemented that promise.

He began by informing himself on agriculture in one of the most exhaustive studies of his life. With his great capacity for concentration and his ability to grasp ideas and thoughts, he went into every detail of his state's greatest industry, the only billion dollar industry in Missouri.

His phenomenal memory stood him in good stead in pursuing this study of agricultural problems. He consulted men

STUART SYMINGTON

who knew various phases of the subject, pored over books, government reports, farm journals, everything that bore on the topic. He informed himself not only on American agriculture, but became familiar with foreign trends, production, and other matters relative.

He fought for, and in 1956 was appointed to, membership in the Senate Committee on Agriculture and Forestry, and was publicly lauded in the Senate for his interest in the farmer. When he went into the Senate he was no better informed than most city men on the problems and questions facing agriculture. Today he is one of the four or five leading experts on agriculture in the Senate, whose judgments, ideas, and advice are most sought for by agricultural people.

One of his battles was with Ezra Taft Benson, Secretary of Agriculture. It happened during the serious drought that occurred in the Midwest in the summer of 1956.

Touring Missouri that year he saw the intensity of the dry spell, and appealed for Federal aid on an emergency basis for the farmers who were "struggling against bankruptcy." He forwarded to the Department of Agriculture a report he had caused to be drawn up on the drought conditions, showing how dairymen and cattle raisers were acutely affected, the drought causing the sale of many foundation herds, and forcing the sale of many farms.

At last, on October 10, while Secretary Benson was campaigning for the Republican Party, he met with the State Drought Committee at Columbia, Missouri, and promised a quick decision on the request for aid for farm ponds, pasture seeding, and assistance in the purchase of grain and hay for starving herds.

But he apparently forgot the promise, for no decision was made as promised.

The emergency was real and acute, but for some reason the Department of Agriculture, which had favored other states, turned down Missouri's appeal.

Symington went on the floor of the Senate January 17, 1957, in a speech in which he said: "We of Missouri do not understand this refusal, because this type and character of assistance was designed and authorized by Congress for just such an emergency."

The following day the Department of Agriculture designated twenty-eight Missouri counties for FHA emergency credit because of drought—the first action taken after nearly seven months of the arid spell, to assist the state's disaster-stricken farmers.

This was a step in the right direction, but other areas needed help just as badly. Symington demanded why Missouri was refused aid when other states were being given extensive assistance, and during his inquiry discovered that the Department of Agriculture had no written regulations of any kind for judging comparative severity of drought conditions. Apparently assistance was being extended on a completely arbitrary basis.

That was contrary to every principle of Symington's thought. Under his demand the Department of Agriculture subsequently—and belatedly—adopted regulations which covered such questions, but though the Missouri drought was broken by spring rains in 1957, as one publication wryly said, "Once again, despite the continuing efforts of Senator Symington and other members of the Missouri delegation, the Department of Agriculture's assistance to farmers suffering from natural disaster had been 'too little, too late.' "

There was another battle, that over a high-handed effort by Benson to change the long-established and well-proven farmer

committee system for administering farm programs in each
county. Soon after he took office as part of the Republican
administration in 1953, the Secretary of Agriculture issued a
series of arbitrary directives stripping farmer committees of
much authority, and ordering them to hire "office managers"
for administrative control. Work time of elected committeemen was reduced, and an unsuccessful attempt made to limit
their terms of office.

In Missouri the administration of the farm program at once
became a political spoils system for the Republicans. The
Republican-controlled state committee began to discharge
elected farm committeemen and replace them with "deserv-
ing" Republicans, in a drive to gain control of some 4,300 jobs
of the kind in the state.

After repeated requests for an investigation of this situation made to Secretary Benson, the two Missouri Senators,
Symington and Hennings, brought the matter to the attention
of the Senate and asked a full investigation.

But the abuses continued, in Missouri and elsewhere.
Farmer-elected committeemen were suspended, or fired, and
fundamental American hearing and appeal procedures were
ignored. Sometimes the charges were trumped up, sometimes
the committeemen were dismissed simply for alleged failure
to "cooperate" with the state Republican chairman.

On July 29, 1955, in a speech on the Senate floor, Symington again called for action, saying, "Two and a half years
would seem to be a sufficient period of time for correction of
any such mess!"

The result was a hearing before the Senate Agriculture
Subcommittee on Farmer Committees, held in Jefferson City,
Missouri. Although not a member of the subcommittee,

Senator Symington attended and took an active part in every session.

When, in June 1956, the hearings were transferred to Washington, Symington had become a member of the Senate Agriculture and Forestry Committe, and so sat into the hearings by right.

It was brought out that an overwhelming percentage of the suspensions—29 per cent—had occurred in Missouri. The subcommittee found that the Missouri situation led to "administration excesses, disruptions, abuses, increased costs and attempts at political control." A general review was recommended.

Symington did not for one day relax his pressure on the Department of Agriculture to review each suspension and dismissal, clear the unjustly accused, grant full hearings for committeemen desiring them, restore the right of those cleared, and ask optional use only of "office managers."

Finally action came. A ruling was made June 11, 1956, that the removal of three Boone County committeemen was "not supportable," and the charges against them "not sustained." Reinstatement was ordered, and the state committee warned against any more such arbitrary actions. Other hearings followed with equally good results.

During the hearings, Secretary Benson wrote a letter to Senator Symington which read, in part:

> I strongly commend the efforts of Senator Humphrey's Subcommittee in focusing attention on situations in the farmer committee system that warranted scrutiny.

Senator Hubert Humphrey of Minnesota was the chairman of the committee in question, but it was Symington, and Benson well knew it, who had done the major work of focusing the spotlight on the Missouri abuses and bringing them forward for investigation and report.

5

It is no secret that there is little love lost between Ezra Taft Benson and Symington, yet Symington has supported every measure of Benson's which he considered constructive and worthwhile.

A man of action is never free from spiteful criticism and actions, and Symington has his foes. None of them are foes due to any dishonorable act. As for his great multitude of friends they, as Edward Stuyvesant Bragg said of Grover Cleveland, "love him for the enemies he has made."

Symington is sensitive by nature, and false or unjust accusations hurt him. But he is learning not to be too thin-skinned. One episode that rankled, however, was a curious persecution by a Missouri judge.

During his first campaign, in 1952, Judge George H. Moore asked a federal grand jury to investigate "conspiracy aspects" of Symington's campaign funds. The grand jury heard the evidence and found no irregularities. Four years after this Judge Moore again asked a grand jury to investigate the same matter, and once more there was not the slightest evidence of irregularities. Both times Sidney Maestre, treasurer, and Jacob M. Lashly, chairman of the Citizens for Symington committee, were called and questioned.

It exasperated Symington, and for a peculiar reason.

"I don't know what it is that Judge Moore has against me," he says. "I don't suppose it really matters. The point is he apparently had it in for me, really had it in for me. So he called these grand jury hearings, and all that came out of them was a clean bill of health for the committee that had worked for me.

"But the thing that many people especially resented and the reason why so many felt it was nothing more than a surreptitious persecution was that if you went all over Missouri and picked ten men whose standing would be highest, therefore the best to handle your money in any campaign, Mr. Lashly and Mr. Maestre unquestionably would be listed in those first ten.

"Mr. Lashly, without any reservation of any kind, is the leading lawyer of St. Louis, a truly great man and a real Christian gentleman. Mr. Maestre is the biggest banker in the state, a man of outstanding integrity, and a Republican, which proves the strength of his convictions.

"What happened was that the motives and honesty and very nature of these people were attacked. What made me feel so terrible was that it really was more an attack on their integrity than mine, because they were handling the money and I wasn't."

Finally, on July 30, 1956, the *St. Louis Globe-Democrat*— the Republican newspaper in St. Louis, published an editorial both forthright and courageous:

PERSECUTION OF A PUBLIC SERVANT

Federal Judge George H. Moore, addressing the grand jury on May 2, 1956, asked it to investigate the conspiracy aspects of the 1952 primary and general election in which Stuart Symington was elected to the United States Senate.

This would be a reasonable enough request, except for the following facts:

A federal grand jury, under Judge Moore, in 1952, and calling almost exactly the same witnesses, made a similar investigation and found no irregularities.

A committee of the United States Senate, in the same year, made a similar investigation with the same results.

One might well ask why, almost four full years after the campaigns, should the same question be rehashed?

Have any new issues been raised? There is no indication of them.

Have any new witnesses come forward? There have been none.

The only circumstances which has changed from the earlier inquiries is that Stuart Symington is now prominently mentioned as a possible Democratic nominee for the Presidency, and the rehashing of old, cold facts at this significant hour appears to be a deliberate attempt by Federal Judge George H. Moore, whose personal animus against Senator Symington is well known, to embarrass Mr. Symington on the eve of the convention.

* * *

The *Globe-Democrat* is not interested in furthering the Presidential candidacy of Mr. Symington. We were one of the first newspapers in the Nation to urge the nomination and election of Gen. Eisenhower. We believe he has been a superb President and we hope he is re-elected.

What does cause us the gravest concern, however, is the persecution of people in the public service and those associated with them.

Senator Symington, for almost four years, has rendered notable and distinguished service to the people of Missouri and the United States.

Sidney Maestre, chairman of the board of the Mercantile Trust Company, who was treasurer of the Citizens for Symington primary campaign, is one of the most universally beloved and respected men ever to live in St. Louis.

Jacob M. Lashly, prominent lawyer and former president of the American Bar Association, the highest honor that can come to a lawyer, was chairman of that campaign.

Mr. Maestre and Mr. Lashly have both been called to testify twice, without any evidence that there were new questions to be answered or new witnesses to be heard. Such questioning inevitably casts a shadow, however unjustified, upon the spotless reputations of Mr. Maestre and Mr. Lashly. And there are others.

* * *

The American Constitution forbids the retrial of a person who has previously been acquitted. By inference, at least, the same should obtain in investigations, unless there is substantial new evidence.

Thus it becomes pure persecution of a public servant, and that is reprehensible.

How can we hope to enlist outstanding men for public service, or have good citizens assist in their election, if they face the knowledge that they may be called upon, time and again, to answer the same charges which were twice found groundless— and that such likelihood grows as they approach the summit of national prominence?

Judge Moore, who will be 79 next Jan. 20, has made many notable contributions to the national scene in his long and distinguished career. He causes great public concern, however, with the obvious rewarming of old inquiries on the eve of a national convention.

The vast need of America is for her ablest and most distinguished sons and daughters to enter the service of the city, state and nation. Have we furnished much incentive to this end in the current Symington investigation?

The resentment of Senator Symington in this case was not for himself, but for the men who supported him who, he feels were hectored and annoyed without any good reason.

"That was quite an editorial," he says of the *Globe-Democrat's* utterance. "It took a great deal of courage on their part, and that ended my problem, because it brought the whole thing out to light and set things straight."

XII

THE McCARTHY ORDEAL

1

The most dramatic, and at the same time unpleasant, episode in Symington's first term as Senator, came in 1954 when the disgraceful episode, called the "Army-McCarthy hearings," took place before a nation-wide television hook-up.

Senator Joseph McCarthy of Wisconsin was at the time at the height of his mud-slinging, gutter-fighting, name-calling, stentorian-lunged career as a self-appointed fanatical "discoverer" of Communists in Government office. He had converted his Investigations Committee into an instrument of power, running it virtually as a one-man show, and keeping the national stage with such virulence and violence that he convinced not a few credulous persons that anyone who took issue with him was a "Communist" for that reason alone, and therefore a traitor to his country. He spent hundreds of thousands of dollars of the taxpayers' money in his junketings; and with his lengthy bellowings and revilings of conscientious and honest men who happened to disagree with him, attracted to himself the kind of attention a demagogue always arouses.

In 1954 he had so succeeded in making of himself a figure who disdained authority, considered himself above the law, did not scruple to distort facts in his favor, and indulged in the most insulting abuse of his victims under the protection of his Senatorial immunity from legal or personal reprisal, that hardly a person on the political scene dared to come to grips with him; because whatever the outcome, the one who did so was sure to emerge covered with filth.

One of those who had not feared to speak out against him was Symington. He has an almost passionate belief in the principle of freedom of speech and of the press, as one of the great—possibly the greatest—of the guarantees of American liberties. And he felt that McCarthy, by his misuse of privilege and power in burying anyone who took issue with him under a load of invective and accusations of disloyalty to America, was stultifying free expression.

He had defended some of McCarthy's victims in public utterances, and speaking at Radcliffe College, Cambridge, Massachusetts, June 10, 1953, he said:

"I am becoming concerned . . . about the fear of the power, and the recklessness, of some of those engaged in the search for Communists and Communist influence. . . .

"Fear itself is corrosive. Fear and freedom cannot co-exist.

"No man is free if he fears his exercise of freedom's rights.

"No man is free if he worries lest one of his friends be called into question, and thereby he himself be exposed to the process of inquisition.

"Freedom is dead for the loyal citizen who nevertheless fears a knock at the door.

"I am deeply disturbed when I encounter American citizens of blameless character and unquestioned loyalty who confess they fear to enter a debate or take a position not in conformity with the views of certain political leaders, because of the fancied danger that they might be thought suspect. . . .

"No thoughtful person can escape the conclusion that there have been, and are, abuses in the exercise of power by committees of Congress . . . and that these abuses are largely responsible for the jeopardy in which the courage of our people has been placed. . . .

"There is no room in this country for dictatorial power, whether it be exercised by a legislator, a Government official, or a ruler. There is no place in our democracy for a Grand Inquisitor.

"We can and we must search out Communism and fight it to its death—but we must do this with the weapons of democracy, democratically applied."

He did not mention McCarthy in that speech. But McCarthy, on reading it, "tried on the shoe"—and found it fitted him like a glove.

Having stated his opinion, Symington expected McCarthy to attack him, and was prepared for it. As it turned out the issue was brought to a focus, when the Army charged that McCarthy, Chairman of the Permanent Subcommittee on Investigations, his counsel Roy Cohn, and his executive director Francis Carr, "had sought by improper means preferential treatment for one Pvt. G. David Schine."

That was the real issue that was to be heard before the committee, but McCarthy and his staff lashed back, with their usual tactics, alleging in forty-six separate counter-charges that the action was brought "to force discontinuance of further attempts by the [Investigations] Committee to expose Communist infiltration in the Army."

Under this typical change of ground, the situations were in a sense reversed. Though Schine, the spoiled son of a rich man, who believed anything could be bought with money, was the object of the investigation, McCarthy's counterattack made the Army of the United States the real victim.

The committee appointed to investigate the charges included four Republican Senators: Karl Mundt of South Dakota, chairman, Everett Dirksen of Illinois, Charles Potter of Michigan, and H. C. Dworshak of Idaho. McCarthy was the regular chairman, but because he was involved in the charges he did not sit as a member—officially, at least.

There were three Democratic Senators: John McClellan of Arkansas, Henry Jackson of Washington, and Stuart Symington of Missouri.

It might have been expected that the Republican majority would do its share to uphold the integrity of the Army, which so suddenly became the whipping boy for McCarthy's malice. President Eisenhower's distaste for the tactics of the Senator from Wisconsin was well known—and also the curious fact that the Chief Executive had not been able to protect his high place from the surging overflow of the man who hoped by arousing mob emotions to make himself President.

There were some, indeed, who believed that McCarthy considered himself already a sort of second President. The *New York Times* said openly:

> There are quite a few politicians who believe that the Administration is rapidly running out of opportunities on which it can grasp the initiative and fight it out once and for all with the junior Senator from Wisconsin.

But as it turned out during the intense and highly publicized hearings, the Republican majority of the committee was so bulldozed and dominated by McCarthy—who actually took over the *de facto* role of chairman, to which the real chairman, Mundt, meekly surrendered—that it was worse than useless in upholding the integrity of the Army from a ferocious and unprecedented attack.

It devolved upon the Democrats to carry the burden of the fight and on none more heavily than on Stuart Symington.

Symington is gentlemanly, courteous, polite, and considerate even of his opponents. He did not relish or want a pigsty battle such as this encounter with McCarthy was sure to be, and all the more so since he did not regard himself as a rough-and-tumble debater, in the sense that the word-spewing, epithet-hurling Wisconsin Senator was.

McCarthy would be in his element, the atmosphere he loved, which appealed to his peculiar nature, since the "investigation" was to be conducted before a nation-wide television audience, with millions of people looking in on the proceedings, hearing the slurs and insults, watching the winces and anguish of decent men as the acknowledged master of bullying tactics, McCarthy, scored in his ugly manner on all who opposed him.

But in the end it was Symington, whose loyalty to his country and concern for its armed forces made him enter the distasteful battle of invective, who was the most effective and at times it seemed the only one who would stand up and throw McCarthy's words in his teeth. It was he who saw how disastrous to the morale of the Army would be the smears and abuse and indignities, which would be aired all over the nation.

So he ranged himself man-to-man against McCarthy, the master of insult, the great shifter of base, the appealer to the mob. And in the fight that followed he showed himself to be a man who would not back off from a fight, however costly; a tough, unterrified adversary, who in spite of his inexperience in such matters became to the television audience the real protagonist of the opposition to McCarthy.

Symington went into the battle knowing that what he was doing might hurt him politically. He was warned by his friends of the rabid nature of certain McCarthy followers, but he did not consider his own interests, political or otherwise, in this crisis. He set his will to save the integrity of the armed forces from a man who would have destroyed that integrity for his own selfish ends.

Each morning as he left for the hearings, Eve Symington reminded him to keep his temper; but sometimes that temper flared under the raw abrasions of McCarthy's innuendo and invective, and there were sharp clashes. He would go home at night, miserable at his own failures, and scold himself for not better following her advice.

Wrote Michael Straight of Symington in *Trial By Television:*

> He knew that he had compromised his ambition, but his ambition itself was changing. In the smoke and dust of this encounter the image of the White House grew dim. He felt that if he went down and took McCarthy with him, he would have served well.

In the arena of the committee hearings, made into a national spectacle by the television cameras, he at first sometimes seemed unready in the debates, and some of his friends were disappointed in his showing. He was not glib enough, he did not equal McCarthy in insulting personalities, he appeared at times confused.

They hoped that he would obliterate McCarthy with one blow, but the dramatics were all with McCarthy. Symington had to persevere, and perseverance is sometimes dull.

What those friends and the viewing public to a great extent missed in those days was the deadly, unswerving determination of the man to reach a certain goal, and bring certain things out of the obscurity of the tangle of charges, counter-charges, threats, and implications against characters and motives, with which McCarthy was clouding the issue.

That Symington suffered in those days there can be no question. His work, no matter how hard, has always been enjoyable to him; the more difficult the task undertaken, the greater the pleasure.

But in these hearings there was no enjoyment. A man with honor, patriotism, and self-respect, he knew himself to be "fighting downhill" as Sam Houston once expressed it. It was a battle of logic against casuistry, manners against vulgarity, the gentleman against the boor. And in any such contest he could not escape being smeared with the muck and filth of a gutter battle. But he committed himself to the fight, and saw it through to the bitter end.

Furthermore, as the hearings went on, Symington grew stronger and gained confidence, becoming more effective day by day.

2

The real issue in McCarthy's fight against the Army before the Committee, obscured so that the public almost lost sight of it and some of the members of the Committee itself seemed to wholly forget it, was shocking and shameful. It was the fact that McCarthy, and his counsel, Roy Cohn, a brash youngster of twenty-seven, swollen with power, had misused that power for the purpose of overturning the whole authority and tradition of the United States Army, in gaining special favors, excuse from ordinary duties of a soldier, and in seeking an unearned commission for G. David Schine, a not very admirable young man, whose father owned a hotel system, and who believed that anything could be obtained through the influence money could bring to bear.

Schine was a pal of Cohn's. They were the same age, and were both sons of wealthy parents. In behalf of Schine, at Cohn's request, McCarthy chose to wield the threat of his feared bludgeon—the so-called "investigation for Communists and Communist influence" which he held over the heads of every Government institution.

Cohn, as the intimate and counsel of McCarthy, held a position of power fascinating to Schine's somewhat adolescent mind. It was only natural perhaps that Schine gravitated to the terrifying McCarthy subcommittee as a "consultant" and "expert on psychological warfare," to which his qualifications were not noteworthy by any standards. For a time he enjoyed this position, and then, suddenly, he was notified that he had been drafted for the Army.

But this was ridiculous! G. David Schine a mere G.I.? Something had to be done about that. With the aid of Cohn he got entree to the Pentagon—where no other draftee ever went on a similar errand—and with complete effrontery proposed that he be sworn in as a commissioned officer, without further preliminaries.

The Pentagon failed to be properly thrilled by this offer, and did not accede.

But there were higher echelons. Robert Stevens, a well-meaning but inept Eisenhower supporter, had been appointed Secretary of the Army. Stevens was summoned to the Schine apartment in New York—and, amazingly, he went. There it was suggested by Schine and Cohn that he take Schine into his office as a "special assistant"—thus placing the hotel tycoon's son beyond the reach of the detested draft board.

Stevens—at that time apparently not fully realizing the powers he was daring—indicated an opinion that Schine ought to go ahead and serve as a private like all the other 430,000 American young men drafted that year.

In spite of "money and influence" Schine found himself inducted into the Army as a private—but by no means an ordinary private.

The efforts to get him an unearned commission still continued. In the meantime, he sought special favors, and offered "inducements"—like trips to Florida—varied by implied threats, to gain them. When this failed, he telephoned his friends on Capitol Hill, and his commanding officers received orders to excuse him from such menial tasks as kitchen police and other unpleasant chores of army life.

Cohn used every form of tactics to gain his friend a commission. It became a sort of an obsession with him, to judge by the evidence. High officers were approached, and every pressure applied. But in the end—to the everlasting credit, in the final analysis, of the Army—no commission was forthcoming for Private G. David Schine.

But while this was going on, be it confessed with shame, he "was treated as no other private had ever been treated before." He was released from drill and work details, and on every week end and holiday received passes, when other trainees got passes only on Christmas or New Year's. At times he simply went A.W.O.L. without a pass, secure in the confidence (not without reason) that he would not be punished as other G.I.'s would have been.

All this, according to the complaint filed by "the Department of the Army," was because Schine's friends "intervened persistently" in his behalf. But the really disgraceful thing about it was that McCarthy and Cohn did not "intervene" as individuals. They intervened as chairman and counsel of the inquisitorial Subcommittee on Investigations, and under that authority they made their demands, and sometimes "used the subcommittee to harass the Army when their demands were not fully satisfied."

It was this wretched distortion of power that was the true point at issue, and this is what Symington labored to bring out of all the confusion of counteraccusations and abuse into focus, during those weeks of the hearings beginning April 22, 1954.

For a time it appeared that McCarthy—who against every rule of procedure and courtesy proceeded to take full control of the hearings, like an accused man before the bar sitting as his own judge—would succeed in keeping this basic issue buried under an avalanche of countercharges meant to turn the whole course of the hearings.

McCarthy had asserted that Schine would not have been drafted "except because of the fact that he worked for my committee."

With that as his position, he proceeded to direct all the force of the inquisition at the Army and its heads. He alleged that he had announced "his determination to pursue [his Army] investigations to the point of calling those . . . responsible for the clearing of Communists. Secretary Robert Stevens then commenced a series of efforts to interfere . . . with the investigations, stop hearings."

To this he added sensational accusations of "bribery," "blackmail," "threats," "protecting Communists infiltrating and protecting Communists who had infiltrated," and "bad faith."

The first rounds were McCarthy's but then there came a serious exposé of his methods. A picture was introduced showing Stevens and Schine apparently in close and smiling conversation before an airforce plane, to prove that "Mr. Stevens was not only solicitous of Private Schine . . . but asked to be photographed with Private Schine," in Cohn's words.

Next day another photograph was produced by the Army's counsel, Joseph Welch, which showed a group including Stevens and Schine—but not alone—and which conclusively proved that the first picture, introduced by McCarthy had been "doctored" by a photographer's trick, so that the other figures were taken out and it appeared that the Secretary and Schine were alone, grinning amiably at each other.

McCarthy tried to intervene with a cry "completely false," and Symington leaned across the table, pounded it, and shouted that he was out of order.

It was a damaging piece of evidence, showing trickery on McCarthy's part, and on the part of his counsel, Roy Cohn. The actual photomontage, it came out, was done by one of McCarthy's men, Don Surine. Symington demanded that Surine be called to testify, and McCarthy's hate exploded in the hottest encounter of the hearings. Afterward, McCarthy met Symington in the corridor and threatened that if Surine were called, McCarthy would "counter with a full-scale smear of Symington."

Symington simply turned and coldly walked away. "I have a bad habit of saying nothing but the truth," he remarked. "A threat like that didn't scare me a bit."

On went the hearings. Secretary Stevens was pilloried and made to look weak and foolish, and very much afraid of McCarthy and his methods, to the point where he tried to curry friendship. He even ran errands for Schine. On one occasion Cohn, bumptious with self-importance and furious that he was asked to remain outside a secret Army installation,

exclaimed: "This is war! We will now *really* investigate the
Army!" And Stevens sent a very humble apology to that
unlicked cub.

General Ralph Zwicker, hero of the Battle of the Bulge,
but for whom, according to Eisenhower, the war might have
turned against the Allies, had been told by McCarthy that
he was "not fit to wear that uniform," during a previous
hearing, and Eisenhower—just back from a golf-playing vacation—had asked the subcommittee to sign a statement that
in the future Army witnesses would not be abused. This statement McCarthy and Dirksen refused to sign, and the *New
York Times* commented:

> Whether President Eisenhower realizes it or not, Senator
> McCarthy is now sharing with him the command of the Army.

Now, triumphantly secure in his defiance of the President,
McCarthy sat in the hearing and bullied Secretary Stevens
and others of the Army almost past bearing.

Symington, a businessman himself, who had made sacri-
fices to serve the Government, feared that the televised hearings would so bring home the cost in labor unrewarded and
fear of humiliation to those in Government, that men of
ability and self-respect would not enter public life. He put a
question along that line, and was answered by pert Roy Cohn:

"We did not make these . . . smear charges against Mr.
Stevens. He made them against us. I assume no responsibility
in that regard."

The McCarthy wrecking crew cared not what it did so long
as it rode supreme.

4

More and more the personal dislike of McCarthy for Symington appeared as the hearings continued, with an increase

of taunts and insults by the Wisconsin Senator. Once he sneer-
ingly called Symington "Sanctimonious Stu" because the latter had made a simple statement of his fundamental belief
in fair play and justice.

He brought up and rehashed some of the old, cold charges
he had made during Symington's 1952 campaign, including
the old Sentner episode.

Symington answered with perfect composure, telling the
facts of the union negotiation under the Wagner act, and
added that the people had paid little attention to McCarthy
when he broadcast all those charges in 1952, and would pay
no attention to them now.

"This is no question of politics," he said. "It is a question
of the loyalty and integrity of the armed forces. . . . For the
first time in our history our people have been urged to entertain serious doubts as to the dedication and loyalty of our
armed forces, from top to bottom. . . . But the vilification has
not stopped with the United States Department of Defense.
Millions of Americans have been told by Senator McCarthy
that this Republican Administration has added a year of
treason to our proud history.

"I am a Democrat, but first and foremost I am an American. It is little comfort to me that these terrible charges are
directed against a Republican Administration, Republican
officials, and our Republican Commander-in-Chief.

"It would appear that some of us want to end up this
country with just plain anarchy."

McCarthy sought to get around that by sneering that he
was "rather amused to hear Senator Symington worrying
about the Republicans." But the point had been tellingly
made, and from this time on Symington began to pin more
and more embarrassing facts on McCarthy and his staff.

Clashes between the men continued. Once when, in his typical manner, McCarthy implied cowardice to Symington, the Missouri Senator turned, looked him fairly in the eye, and replied:

"You said something about being afraid. I want you to know from the bottom of my heart that I'm not afraid of anything about you, or anything you've got to say, any time, any place, anywhere."

For once McCarthy found himself without any ready rejoinder. He was looking into the eyes of a real fighting man, and he knew it.

Wrote Michael Straight of this:

There were few other men in public life in this land of the free who could truthfully say in 1954 that they were not afraid of McCarthy.

At another time, during an exchange in which McCarthy had been especially vicious, Symington said to him, almost with a look of pity:

"You ought to see a psychiatrist."

There were cheers in many an American heart when that very pertinent suggestion to McCarthy went out over the television.

5

It was the Democrats in the committee who upheld the Executive against the encroachments of McCarthy and the Legislative branch.

Toward the end Symington pinpointed the carelessness of the security procedures of McCarthy's staff, which might give an enemy agent the very thing McCarthy was talking about, access to government secrets.

"You're attempting by innuendo to smear my staff!" exclaimed McCarthy.

"Not at all," said Symington, and continued his questioning of the witness then before the committee, Francis Carr, McCarthy's special agent.

At the conclusion he faced his adversary, and said over the microphone, to millions listening in and to McCarthy himself:

"In all the years that I have been in government, based on the testimony given to this committee under oath, I think the files of what you call 'my staff, my director, my chief-of-staff' are the sloppiest and most dangerously handled files I have ever heard of."

The audience in the hearing room burst into spontaneous applause, and the chairman had to use his gavel to restore order.

Eventually Symington and his colleagues of the Democratic membership of the committee succeeded in bringing the hearing exactly to where McCarthy did not want it—the use of the Subcommittee power to gain improper privileges for Private G. David Schine.

That was where the hearings ended, with everyone worn to the bone. At the finish Senator McClellan summed the whole thing up in these words:

"The series of events that . . . made these hearings mandatory will be recognized and long remembered as one of the most disgraceful episodes in the history of our government. . . . Simply to say that this series of events is regrettable is a gross understatement. They are deplorable and unpardonable. There is no valid excuse and justification for this situation having occurred and it will now become our solemn duty to fix the responsibility."

The results of this hearing are history.

They marked, for one thing, the high tide of McCarthy and McCarthyism. From the day they ended his power and prestige decreased.

The hippodrome before the television cameras, with all its ugly atmosphere of billingsgate, sneering, and shouted accusations and slurs, showed to the American people the irresponsible exercise of terrorism by a fanatic who also was an egomaniac. It displayed the august gentlemen of the Senate in the light of mud-spattered brawlers in some filthy back alley.

The responsibility was McCarthy's for bringing about the shameful exhibition, and for setting its tone. That it hurt him there can be no question.

As Symington said to him during one of their sharp exchanges, "The American people have had a look at you for six weeks." That look was not pleasing to the fair-minded and thinking people.

The hearings had some constructive results. They re-emphasized the constitutional separation of powers, clarified the power of Congressional Committees to subpoena officials of other branches of the government, and set areas in which Executive Department communications are privileged and may not be inquired into by Congressional committees.

Furthermore they eliminated one-man hearings in the future, separated files of committees from those of individual Senators, and showed the need to establish rules preventing intimidation of Government officials by members of Congressional committees.

Finally, they aroused the Senate to a realization of how the whole body had been demeaned by the actions of one self-willed member.

Even before the Army hearings, McCarthy had been the object of criticism. Senator William Benton of Connecticut introduced a resolution to determine whether or not McCarthy should be expelled from the Senate as early as 1951. Early in 1952 a Senate subcommittee reported that McCarthy had been "motivated by self-interest" in some of his personal and political actions, but was entitled to keep his seat.

During the Army hearings, Senator Ralph E. Flanders, Republican, of Vermont made a speech in which he introduced into the Senate a resolution to censure McCarthy for conduct unbecoming a Senator.

McCarthy fought it by all the means in his power, but a select committee of the Senate, headed by Senator Arthur Watkins, Republican, of Utah, voted to censure him on two counts, and criticize him on three others.

Then, in December, the entire Senate sitting as a body, after various parliamentary moves, voted overwhelmingly, 67 to 22, to condemn McCarthy solemnly for his conduct toward Senate committees.

It was a shattering blow to his prestige and pride. Thereafter he gradually faded out of prominence until his death of a sudden illness May 2, 1957.

XIII

A "FAVORITE SON"
AND THE DEFENSE ISSUE

1

The most serious thing in Stuart Symington's life is the safety of the United States of America. His other interests in government are wide, but this, in the critical age in which we now live, is to him the most vital of all matters involving the Nation.

In the spring of 1956 a situation developed which offered two interesting alternatives—personal ambition or a service to the country.

As a result of Symington's long insistence, the Senate at last decided to investigate fully the state of the preparedness of the United States for a global, nuclear war. On February 24, 1956, Senator Richard B. Russell, Chairman of the Armed Services Committee, named a Subcommittee on the Air Force.

Its chairman, the only logical choice for the position because of his acknowledged experience and study, was Symington. Other members were two Democrats, Henry M. Jackson, Washington, and Sam J. Ervin, North Carolina; and two Republicans, Leverett Saltonstall, Massachusetts, and James H. Duff, Pennsylvania.

The following day the directive for the hearings was given Symington by Russell. After some weeks devoted to gathering information and evidence, and expert witnesses to testify, the hearings began on April 16, and continued for a considerable period.

In the meantime, something of great personal interest to the Chairman of the Subcommittee took place. In the midst of the Air Force hearings the Missouri state Democratic convention met, and on May 28, by unanimous vote, pledged the state delegation to the Democratic National convention to nominate and vote for Stuart Symington as the party's nominee for President. He had not asked for this favorite son action, which was spontaneous, but he soon found that it was taken more than a little seriously in many quarters.

There was a three-cornered battle for the party's national nomination, between Adlai Stevenson, Estes Kefauver, and Averell Harriman. Though Stevenson had the inside track, Kefauver had made an impressive pre-convention campaign and had many delegates, and Harriman also was strong both in delegates and with the support of Harry Truman.

In such a situation there was believed to be a good prospect of a stalemate in the convention, and national magazines and newspapers suddenly began to pay considerable attention to Symington as the best of all dark horse candidates.

Appraising him, the *Saturday Evening Post* said:

> So far, Symington has rigorously—and wisely, his friends believe—put down efforts to start an organized Presidential boom for him. But his name has been discussed with increasing frequency in the Democratic hierarchy and one of the party's ablest pulse takers recently made a quiet series of probing trips through key sections of the country that impressed him with Symington's potentialities at the grass roots.

Such straws in the wind do not capture a Presidential nomination. They merely indicate strong or weak points or what might happen, when and if. For example, Symington as a compromise candidate has been the subject of much favorable comment in Southern, and more recently border states.

But . . . he has diligently avoided being linked with the Southern bloc in Congress, while assiduously cultivating the ground for a future yield of votes in other areas. For example, he is generally regarded with favor and, in some instances, with enthusiasm among the nation's top labor leaders. His contacts in the business world are probably broader than any other potential candidate's and his business experience has varied from manual labor in the shops to top executive posts in big companies. He has a background of effective administration service in no less than six important Government jobs. He represents a Midwestern farming state and he was strongly supported by Negro voters in his only election contest so far.

. . . If the Democrats do get around to the junior Senator from Missouri when they are making up their collective mind at Chicago, they will at least be assured of plenty of action against the titleholder. And if they don't there is always 1960.

And *Life* magazine had this to say of him in a full-length article complete with pictures, after commenting on the dissident elements in the Democratic Party:

Such a situation would call for a Presidential candidate who can write with both hands, a liberal conservative, a pro-labor businessman, a Southerner who has lived in the North, a civil-righter who will not annoy the South. Symington answers this description—literally. He smashed his left elbow as a youngster and in the long period of recuperation learned to write ambidextrously. He comes from a border state and from a prominent Southern family and has lived half his life in the North. He is a self-made businessman who is popular with labor leaders. As a Senator he ranks as a liberal but is an intimate of the conservative Democratic leaders in Congress.

Symington has run for office only once, but that campaign—

for the Senate in 1952—was impressive. He demonstrated that
he can shake hands like Estes Kefauver. He ran far ahead of
Stevenson on his state ticket. He is no orator, but he is handsome and convincing on TV. Unlike Governor Frank Lausche
of Ohio, he is popular with organization Democrats. Unlike
Governor Averell Harriman of New York, he is completely acceptable to Southern Democrats. It sometimes seems that,
politically speaking, nothing is wrong with him.

There were many other such statements in newspapers and
magazines over the nation, and it added up to what was, as
one publication put it, "something far more substantial than
a favorite son movement."

Symington would hardly have been human had such comments and the genuine interest of some of the leaders of the
party not been important to him. And Symington is a very
human man, with an American's normal ambitions and an
American's great reverence for the lofty post of President.
When he was a boy in a poor family in Baltimore, working
at odd jobs to help out the family exchequer and frequently
going without necessary new clothes when he attended school,
he probably heard the old saying: "Any boy born in America
may some day grow up to become President." It would almost seem that great mutation of fortune might actually be
possible for him in the light of this sudden development.

2

But meantime he was in the midst of the Air Force hearings, and what he was learning was of grave importance to the
Nation. The *Life* article had said further:

Talk of Symington-for-President is especially embarrassing—
and tantalizing—right now. In mid-April, as chairman of a
Senate subcommittee, Symington began a long-delayed investi-

gation of the Air Force and its weapons programs. Every politician knows that if this investigation turns up any shocking facts, the chairman's reputation will soar. Though Symington proposed the investigation more than a year ago, its timing was decided on by other Democratic leaders in the Senate, and the committee's study is scheduled to be completed and its report issued only a few weeks before the Democratic convention. In an election year it is patently impossible to keep politics out of an investigation of air power, including missiles. But Symington has tried commendably, and successfully so far, to keep any Symington-for-President talk in the background.

"Shocking facts" were indeed being developed in the hearings, and they would have made sensational reading in the newspapers in a campaign year. To publish the report would have been an almost irresistible inducement to a run-of-the-mill politician. Stuart Symington was not even tempted.

The hearings were completed July 19, and the Democratic National convention was held in Chicago in mid-August. There would have been ample time for the committee findings to be broadcast to the Nation, together with the name of the man who had made those grave findings possible.

Symington did not issue his report at that time—for what to him was the most impelling of reasons. He felt the report was so important that he did not want it to be brought out in such a way that anyone could discount it as a political document. He literally, for this reason which superseded any thought of self, kept "any Symington-for-President talk in the background."

In the pre-convention days at Chicago, Stanley Fike and Jim Meredith were there but Symington was not. Fike tells his story of the Missourian's attitude and actions as follows:

"I had planned to get some reading done and go over some work on the plane en route to Chicago, but instead started

visiting with a *New York Times* photographer assigned to
cover the convention. He was the first to say what I heard
many times in the ensuing days: 'If the convention doesn't
nominate Stevenson, it will be Symington.' I wanted to check
and see if there was any real basis for these reports.

"I knew, of course, Senator Symington's position. He had
consistently refused to enter any Presidential primaries although invited into seventeen different states for that purpose. For many months he had refused invitations to speak
outside Washington and he had sent back campaign contributions and thanked those who wrote in wanting to help, saying,
'Thanks, but no, I'm not seeking office.'"

Arriving at Chicago, Fike checked into the headquarters for
the Missouri delegation, and then went over to where the Platform Committee was meeting at the Blackstone Hotel.

"There I heard once again," he says, "the statement in
stronger terms: 'If there is a block between Stevenson and
Harriman, it will be Symington. Everyone can agree on him.'
Mrs. Sallie Haley, president of the Missouri Democratic Women's Clubs and a member of the Platform Committee, reported this type of comment being made by committee members from many states. They told her: 'We like your man
Symington,' or 'I'm for Stevenson but if we can't get him,
then I want Symington,' or 'I'm for Harriman, but if he can't
win then I'll be for your man from Missouri, Symington.'"

Fike then visited the convention headquarters at the Con-
rad Hilton Hotel, where the lobbies were filled with milling
delegates, and afterward went to pay his respects to former
President and Mrs. Truman, who had just arrived that morning.

"Already," he says, "the Man from Independence had put
a lot of life into what had been a dull pre-convention period

with his announcement that morning that he would give the name of his candidate in a press conference Saturday afternoon. There was no question that Mr. Truman was enjoying himself immensely. As he said, he just thought he'd liven things up. That he did."

And what was Symington doing in this period of pre-convention activity? He was at Nantucket, Massachusetts, calmly taking a vacation with Mrs. Symington. He might have been moving about among the delegates in Chicago where his personality assuredly would have won him many friends and possible voters, but he had made a resolution and he stayed at Nantucket playing golf, sitting in the sun, resting, while other candidates were feverishly making hay.

Fike spent that Friday morning talking with newspaper men, and answering calls from would-be Symington supporters, wanting to know where the Symington headquarters would be. To these his answer always was, "Sorry, but we have no headquarters and no literature."

That afternoon, however, he received word that Harry Truman wanted Symington to call him at the first opportunity. Fike reached the Senator at Nantucket, and Symington promised to call Truman at eight o'clock next morning, Chicago time. The rest of the day Fike spent with Jim Meredith, explaining over and over to eager questioners the Senator's position: he was not a candidate except as the Missouri delegation wanted him to be. He was not seeking the nomination. He would not seek the nomination. If the convention for any reason decided it wanted him to lead the Democratic Party in the fall, he would do it to the best of his ability. But that was all.

Decidedly it was a most unorthodox position for a man to take under the circumstances. Fike knew the underlying reason: that problem of the defense report which was of such great concern to him.

Saturday morning Symington called Truman at the time agreed, but was told by the hotel that no calls were being accepted. He thereupon went out to play golf.

As it turned out the "no calls" report was a mistake, for Truman already had been out for his walk and was back in his suite by seven-thirty o'clock in the morning, and was anxious to talk to Symington.

That morning Fike devoted to answering questions on the Senator's position on various matters, and repeating the unvarying statement to growing numbers of newspaper, television, and radio reporters: "No, the Senator has no statement to make. His position is clear. He is not a candidate except that the Missouri delegation, under orders from the Missouri State Democratic Convention will place Senator Symington's name in nomination for the Presidency."

That afternoon Truman had the call placed by one of his staff, and after some connection difficulties finally got through to Symington.

"Mr. Truman and Mr. Symington had frequently disagreed," says Fike. "They disagreed strongly when Symington was Secretary of the Air Force as to the number of wings needed. Symington supported seventy wings; the Administration reduced the planned air strength to forty-eight and then forty-two wings. At that point Symington resigned. There were other points on which they took issue. But in spite of these disagreements, Truman and Symington always remained personally friendly. They respect each other both for their agreements and disagreements.

"Knowing this, I was not surprised when I came into the room just as the former President was talking with the Senator, and heard him strongly urging Symington to come out to Chicago as soon as possible. 'The convention is interesting,' he said over the phone. 'It's the place to be if you want to win.' "

With this concrete evidence that Truman really believed Symington was an active factor, Fike also called the Senator and urged him to come out early. Symington, however, did not change his plans and went out just before the opening of the convention.

Meantime Truman had announced his support for Harriman.

When Symington at last arrived in Chicago, to receive an ovation from many of the delegates, he simply said that he was in the hands of the Missouri delegation and told them to do whatever they felt to be right.

In spite of this behavior, which could be interpreted as reluctance, in the balloting that followed Symington received votes from more states than were received by any other favorite son. Adlai Stevenson, of course, was finally nominated.

3

And still the air power report was in Symington's hands. The full transcript of the hearings was, of course, given to the Defense Department, day by day, in case any of the testimony might be utilized for the defense of the nation, and the hearings were public so anyone could attend them, and newspapers carried frequent stories about witnesses and their statements. But the full report, with the findings and recommendations of the committee, had not been released for publication.

In the campaign that fall considerable pressures were placed on him to so release it.

Originally the hearing had been designed only to inquire into the Air Force. But during its sessions its scope had been broadened to include the Navy, which had substantial air power, and also the Army, which had some.

It had been a most thorough hearing, the first real investigation of air power ever made by Congress, and its findings were highly critical of the Republican Administration's inadequacies, delays, and waste, with a corresponding very grave set of findings on the growth of Russian war-making potential.

Again it would have made excellent campaign ammunition —not for Symington this time, but for his party.

And again he decided, on his own conscience, not to release it.

"This is beyond politics," he told friends, "I hope it will awaken the country to what the situation is, and I don't want any hint that it is purely political to weaken it in the public mind."

Because of this he was not entirely popular in some quarters, but he did not waver. The hearings, he said, were nonpolitical in purpose. The information was all in the hands of the Department of Defense, but the findings ought not be used for political reasons now.

Not until the campaign was ended, and the next session of Congress was under way, did Symington release the report with the findings and recommendations. He submitted it to the Chairman of the Committee on Armed Services, January 25, 1957. It was published as Document No. 29 of the 85th Congress, February 20, 1957.

There could be no taint of politics in it then.

XIV

THE WARNING

1

In the period between April 16 and July 19, 1956, over which the Air Force hearings were held, some very eminent men, the most highly qualified experts in their field, testified before the committee.

Among these were General of the Army Omar N. Bradley; General Walter Bedell Smith, of the State Department; Admiral Robert R. Carney; General Carl A. Spaatz, former Chief of Staff of the Air Force; General Curtis E. LeMay, Commander of the Strategic Air Command; Colonel Edward M. Nichols, Director of Operation, SAC; General John P. McConnell, Director of Plans, SAC; Trevor Gardner, former Assistant Secretary of the Air Force for Research and Development; Dr. James R. Killian, Jr., president of the Massachusetts Institute of Technology; General Nathan F. Twining, Air Force Chief of Staff; General Earle E. Partridge, Commander of the Continental Air Defense Command; General Otto P. Weyland, Commander of the Tactical Air Command; Charles E. Wilson, Secretary of Defense; General Maxwell D. Taylor, Army Chief of Staff; Admiral Arleigh Burke, Chief of Naval Operations, and many others, including numerous technical civilian experts of highest standing.

It was a highly imposing list of witnesses, and the testimony they gave all added up to these alarming things: the United States was falling dangerously behind Russia in armament. The United States seemed destined to fall even farther behind in the years to come. The United States under its present Administration was making no adequate effort to change this perilous condition.

This warning was sounded months before the first Russian Sputnik was launched, and public concern and interest consequently aroused.

There was complete agreement among the witnesses that there would be no longer any time for the United States to rely upon its industrial capacity and mobilization base to produce the necessary military strength after a possible war was started.

General Bradley thus expressed it:

"In the past, oceans constituted a barrier to direct attack against our boundaries, and we were able to expand our giant industrial and armed potential even after our entry into war. Thus, with the assistance of our allies, we won two conflicts: World War I and World War II. There is no assurance that time will work for us in the future. In fact, indications are just the opposite. . . . One point should be stressed: to be effective, either as a deterrent, or as a defensive factor, air power must be 'in being.'. . . If it [a war] should come, there is going to be no time to prepare afterward."

The testimony was to the effect that the importance of plant conversion, the value of strategic stockpiles, and the training of manpower after the initial attack had changed entirely under present conditions, were minimized, in fact.

Admiral Carney compared the situation today with the beginning of World War II as follows:

"I think the principal point of difference is that the danger comes from an aggressive potential which might initially be directed to us right off the bat, rather than directed to keeping us out of the conflict.

"The situation is one which would immediately jeopardize the United States, and secondly, there has now come to pass a situation in which attack can be launched against us immediately in a matter of hours.

"This could not happen in former times. That being the case, we must be prepared to resist that attack, and we don't have time to build up, so that the forces, the idea of the forces in being, is of infinitely greater importance today than it has ever been before, and this is true of all services and all arms."

Symington, already fully aware of all this, wanted to get it on the record, and he was throughout the chief questioner, able with his close knowledge to bring out important pieces of testimony which otherwise might have been overlooked or forgotten, but which were necessary to the full picture.

General Twining put the gravity of the situation this way:

"I see no reason to believe that air defense, at any time in the near future, will be able to prevent a well-planned and executed air offensive from inflicting terrible damage on our country. Hence, I believe our survival can be guaranteed only if we maintain in a constant state of readiness a deterrent striking force. It must be so organized, equipped, trained and protected as to insure a capability to deliver a tremendous punishment to any aggressor."

At that time it was agreed that the great deterrent to war with Russia or any other power was the Strategic Air Command, with its long-distance bombers capable of delivering devastating nuclear weapons anywhere in the world from its widely scattered bases.

The whole Free World, indeed, so regarded it, as was shown by a paragraph from one of Winston Churchill's speeches to the British Parliament, quoted by General LeMay:

"The United States Strategic Air Command is a deterrent of the highest order and maintains ceaseless readiness. We owe much to their devotion to the cause of freedom in a troubled world. The primary deterrents to aggression remain the nuclear weapon and the ability of the highly organized and trained United States Strategic Air Command to use it."

It must have given Symington a thrill of pride to hear those words of tribute to an arm of the Air Force, which he had helped in planning and for which he had fought not only as Secretary of the Air Force but since he had come to the Senate.

But what of the SAC, and how long would it remain a potent deterrent?

The facts were depressing. Not only in the development of striking power, but in the training of technicians, the testimony showed that Russia was relentlessly moving ahead of the United States.

Symington himself expressed the latter situation in a question addressed to Admiral Carney:

"Before the Armed Services Committee last year in open hearing, it was testified that in 1950 the Soviet graduated some 20,000 engineers and scientists, and we, 50,000.

"By 1954 these figures were just about reversed. We graduated slightly less than 20,000 and they graduated over 50,000 engineers and scientists.

"Unless something happens with respect to that trend, isn't it almost automatic the way that wars are developing on a technical basis, that we will give up our possible superiority to the Communists?"

To this Admiral Carney replied, "I regret to say so, but I certainly believe it, sir."

And Dr. Killian, of M.I.T. said, "I am convinced that our national security can be jeopardized and even lost, but the mismanagement of our resources—both proved and potential —of creative intelligence.

"There is no doubt that the Soviets have generated a respect and enthusiasm for science and engineering that has operated to give them a larger supply of trained professionals in these fields, from a smaller total school and university population, than is this country's.

"What about the quality of this larger supply then? In many fields it is good; and in the critical scientific areas, first-rate."

As to the striking potential, the picture was as dark, Evidence showed that in aircraft production the Soviet was producing more combat aircraft than the United States, had thousands more aircraft in combat units, was making about ten times as many fighter planes.

Laboring through that April, May, June, and July, Symington and his Committee sought for every available bit of information on what was then (in 1956) still in somewhat the experimental stage, the work on intercontinental ballistic missiles both here and in Russia.

On that dread subject there was no higher expert in its world-wide implications than Symington himself. Nearly two years before, on July 21, 1954, he had solemnly called the Nation's attention to the great new menace in a speech on the Senate floor. On that occasion he began by discussing status of nuclear weapons, pointing out that whereas they were once difficult and expensive to make because of scarcity of material, technology had discovered other more plentiful elements so that they could be manufactured cheaply and in great quantity, enough to threaten the very existence of the entire world.

Then he said, with terrible earnestness:

"The second development of supreme importance to the future security of the United States is this: Within a few years it will be possible to deliver atomic and hydrogen weapons by long-range, intercontinental ballistic missiles, descendants of the old German V-2.

"That weapon was most effective over ten years ago—and it is dangerous to our national security that since when we have not followed the Communists in concentrating on its development.

"But the V-2, the first of these ballistic missiles, was not even a Model T compared to the ICBM's of today. . . .

"These new units of destruction will climb so high, and descend so fast, that they will need protection against destruction by atmospheric friction.

"They will be guided only during the first portion of their climb, but guided so precisely that any error in accuracy can be measured, not in miles, but in hundreds of yards.

"To those listening to the arguments of biased professionals who advocate fighting a possible future war with weapons of the past war—something which never happens—these developments may sound fantastic.

"But the intercontinental ballistic missile is not fantastic at all. . . .

"The incredible destructive power of hydrogen warheads makes it possible to destroy a nation by launching a hail of ballistic missiles against it.

"The effect of such a missile barrage on an entire continent would be comparable to the effect of an ordinary artillery barrage on a few acres of battlefield."

Symington paused to let his words sink in. Then he continued:

"The most ominous aspect of this new weapon, however, is that once launched, there is no defense against it . . . no workable method of intercepting them [ICBM's] or deflecting them has been devised, even in theory.

"There is no doubt whatever that the intercontinental ballistic missiles will be produced in quantity years before any adequate defense against them is worked out.

"Will the Communists have these ICBM's before we do? There are many reasons to believe they will.

"For over thirty years the Russians have been working on rockets—and this type of missile is a logical development of the twin-stage rocket . . .

"We know that, over nine years ago, the Communists captured a number of German scientists who, in addition to working successfully on the V-2, were also designing an ICBM for attack on the United States.

"We can be very sure that these Germans along with the outstanding Soviet scientists, have made much progress in the latter field.

"We also know that over the years we have consistently underrated the ability of the Communists to manufacture superlative new weapons of war in large quantities. . . .

"America has also made progress. But over here our policy is a far cry from the all-out program of the Communists. . . . For years the United States has appropriated less, each year, for research and development, than it did the previous year. . . .

"These two all-important facts—the hydrogen bomb and

the ICBM—are not something in the distant future, to be handled by our children, or our grandchildren.

"They are with us now. They will be with us in great quantity within from five to ten years . . . the time to take stock is not tomorrow, but right now. . . .

"Let us remember that in a short time, primarily because of these two new developments, the United States may be more vulnerable than Great Britain was in the late thirties.

"Let me ask again, as I did in a talk at Baylor University over five years ago: 'Who is behind us today as we were then behind England?'

"If we are attacked tomorrow, and do not have the capacity to retaliate with instant and total devastation, we shall go down in defeat; and freedom will perish from the earth."

A great deal of this is fully known and accepted by the American public today. It was not in 1954. Symington's speech caused a sudden spate of publicity in newspapers and magazines, with articles, illustrations, and diagrams, to inform the people.

2

With a chairman who saw and studied the danger that far ahead and even before, it is not to be wondered that the Committee dug up some uncomfortable facts. While witnesses' estimates varied as to the relative progress of the United States against Russia in the missile field, they were in full agreement that the Reds had made great strides with those weapons and were increasing their pace.

It was brought out that seven years before, the United States had a monopoly on nuclear weapons, but the monopoly no longer existed. Likewise, the superiority of the United States in aerial bomb delivery capacity had disappeared.

In the face of this lag in power, the Republican Administration had pursued a policy of steadily cutting back the money available for defense operation and development. The budget expenditures for the year 1953, 1954, and 1955, were read, together with the budget estimates of the expenditures for the years 1956 and 1957:

1953 defense expenditures were $43.7 billion.
1954 defense expenditures were $40.3 billion.
1955 defense expenditures were $35.5 billion.
1956 defense expenditures (estimated) $35.1 billion.
1957 defense expenditures (estimated) $35.7 billion.

One of the great handicaps presented by the shearing off of appropriations through a ceiling on military funds, was shown to be the loss of trained manpower both in the armed services and in the technical fields. As one of the witnesses said, grimly:

"It is pretty hard to replace a man's brains."

3

The report, when issued, was the first official governmental finding on the new world armament situation, and created a profound sensation. The findings of the Committee, summarized, were as follows:

1. In any future war there will be far less time than ever before in which to mobilize. As a result the importance of "forces in being" has steadily increased to the point where they are now indispensable.

2. The United States had a strong strategic striking force at the time of the inquiry (1956). This was due in large measure, however, to weapons designed, money appropriated, and contracts let many years before; and even this strength

was declining relatively against the steadily growing capacity of the Soviets.

3. The defenses of the United States had been weakened because of the failure to act on national intelligence information; and also because of a tendency to either ignore or underestimate Soviet military progress.

4. The Soviets exceeded the United States in the number of modern combat aircraft in operational units. They were producing more aircraft than the United States. They had decreased the time used between the original design and quantity production of combat aircraft as compared with the time required by the United States.

5. This country had an insufficient number of jet bombers and there was no program to produce a sufficient number.

6. A growing shortage of skilled manpower was resulting in inadequate maintenance of aircraft, and therefore unnecessary accidents and deaths. The manpower shortage increased the inability to maintain a proper state of alert against possible attack.

7. The United States had the capacity to produce an adequate number of jet tankers, but had failed completely to do so, a neglect that seriously decreased the effectiveness of our air power.

8. The decline in strategic striking power of our Air Force as against that of the Soviet could not be overcome significantly by the use of naval air power.

9. The effectiveness of our strategic striking power and air defense was dependent in large measure on an adequate airbase structure. The structure existing afforded neither the alert status, nor that dispersal necessary for security. The deficiency on the continental United States was becoming increasingly dangerous because of the deterioration on overseas base struc-

tures and the growing long-range capability of Soviet aircraft.

10. The vulnerability of the United States to sudden attack had increased greatly in the last decade and this vulnerability would continue to increase in the foreseeable future.

11. The Department of Defense had failed to develop an adequate defense warning system, and the planning of naval strength left the United States vulnerable to submarine attack on our shipping, and to submarine missile attack on targets in the nation itself.

12. The Soviets were rapidly closing the qualitative gap. Yet our qualitative lead was being given as justification for passing over the Soviets' quantitative superiority in military air power.

13. The duplicating approach characteristic of many research and development programs in the Department of Defense, along with dollar limitations placed on such programs, had retarded needed modernization of weapons systems, and retarded significant scientific break-throughs. They contrasted with Soviet policies which produced extraordinary Soviet progress in research and development.

14. The Department of Defense not only permitted duplication, even triplication in the development of missiles, but delayed in giving overriding priority to the ballistic-missile program, with a resulting serious loss of time compared with the Soviets' rapid rise.

15. Financial considerations had often been placed ahead of defense requirements, to the serious danger of our national security, and confusion and inefficiency in defense planning had developed from vacillating policies of first emphasis then de-emphasis with respect to limited war against unlimited war. It was essential that we be prepared for both.

16. The United States had the capacity to produce and

maintain air power stronger than that of the Soviets, but the Department of Defense had not utilized this capacity. Yet, with proper administration this superiority could be maintained without jeopardizing a sound economy and without imposing additional tax burdens on the people.

The seventeenth and last conclusion was illuminating:

"Under our form of government, the American people have not only the right, but also the need, to receive all information about our national defense which would not help a possible enemy. Nevertheless, the public is neither adequately nor accurately informed about our military strength as against the great and growing military strength of the Communists.

"The public has failed to receive from official sources complete, accurate, and timely information which it has the right to know."

4

The report of the Symington committee, in spite of its far-reaching implications, was received in an atmosphere of political apathy by the Defense Department and the Administration. The Distant Early Warning (DEW) line along the arctic circle, and "Texas towers" (fixed radar stations) positioned off the Atlantic coast, were the chief achievements during this period, and both, Symington had warned, were of little use in an ICBM attack.

Then, on October 5, 1957, the electrifying announcement came from Radio Moscow, that Russia had successfully launched into orbit encircling the earth an artificial satellite. This was the first Sputnik. The signals from the Soviet satellite were hear all around the world, and the Sputnik itself was glimpsed as it streaked on its orbit.

It created a profound sensation, and dramatized the serious

relative deterioration of the United States as against the Soviets in the development of ICBM's, accurately described and warned against in the Symington committee's report on its findings.

While the Sputnik itself was not a ballistic missile, it proved beyond question that the Russians possessed both the power plant and the guidance equipment which they had developed for ICBM purposes. Orbiting of the Sputnik demonstrated in spectacular and fearsome manner what many had been unwilling to accept from the factual warning of the Symington report issued the previous February.

Events followed rapidly:

The Soviets began to announce that they now had the intercontinental ballistic missiles to deliver atomic warheads and thus confirmed the worst fears of Symington and the military leaders of the Nation.

That brought from President Eisenhower, on October 9, a statement expressing "concern" that the United States was not "farther ahead" in the production of ICBM's.

November 3, the Soviets announced the launching of a second, larger Sputnik, containing a live dog which continued to exist for some time while the satellite orbited around the earth.

November 7, Eisenhower made a nation-wide radio and television talk "designed to allay fears concerning the Soviet scientific achievements." Significantly, he also announced on the same day the appointment of Dr. Killian of M.I.T., one of the Symington committee's expert witnesses, as his "special assistant in science and technology."

November 8, the day following, Neil McElroy, Secretary of Defense, in a reversal of Administration policy, ordered the United States armed forces to "proceed promptly" with a program to launch earth satellites with the aid of ballistic missile test rockets.

November 13, five days later, Eisenhower in another nation-wide radio and television talk proposed "a considerable in-crease in future defense spending to meet the challenge of scientific advances by the U.S.R.R."

November 30, Eisenhower's "committee on scientists and engineers" warned in a report that "the U.S.R.R. might lead the world in technology in five or ten years unless the United States broadened and strengthenend its own efforts."

By this time the Administration had come a long way around toward accepting and adopting the findings of the Symington committee and was seeking hastily to implement them. The public, now fully aroused, was clamoring for action.

At last the Administration seemed to be showing signs of long-delayed action in the right direction.

The warnings of Stuart Symington were vindicated.

But if he felt any elation, he did not show it. He was too profoundly concerned. The result was very belated. He only hoped that it was not too late.

XV

TO THE PEOPLE
FOR THEIR VERDICT

1

The fall of 1958 brought another election campaign. This time there was no question of the Democratic nominee for the Senate in Missouri, nor indeed was there much question of his election. The only question was the size of the majority he would roll up.

Nothing better showed the difference in the opinion Missouri held of her junior Senator as against that which was held at the beginning of the 1952 campaign, than an editorial in the *Kansas City Star*, a newspaper traditionally Republican in policy. The editorial, published October 14, 1958, ran as follows:

As the Missouri Senatorial situation stacks up, the re-election of Sen. Stuart Symington is as certain as anything political can be. In our opinion, he should be re-elected. Two factors influence our thinking. In times like these, they should be pointed out.

We haven't always agreed with Senator Symington in the past. Often we think he is over-partisan or political in some of his stands—on the farm question, for instance. Nor do we expect to agree with him always in the future. And certainly this carries no implication as to 1960, which will have to be decided on the situation then.

But these are dangerous days for the nation and they will be dangerous for years to come. Missouri's junior Senator has an intelligent understanding of the international situation which few Senators possess. More to the point, he has acquired an expert knowledge of our defense problem in this changing era of Sputniks, missiles, and shots at the moon. He was one of the first to sense that past concepts of defenses are obsolete and out-moded and that the future lay, not altogether, but basically, in the air.

There are those who think that Symington is an extremist on defense. Not once, but several times, his recommendations have gone beyond those of the military command. But one thing is dead certain. If there is going to be any mistake in this field, it is better to err on the side of defense and over-expansion than to underplay it.

This thorough knowledge in an intricate area created by the atomic and missile age is needed now in Washington as never before . . .

Symington has the broad understanding of the times which enables him to make his particular contribution to the national defense. These days are too perilous to put partisan considerations above an obvious contrast in choice before Missouri.

That, of course, is the overriding reason why Symington should be re-elected. But there is another consideration, a lesser and more selfish one. Both Missouri Senators happen to live in St. Louis. On the many problems that arise from Kansas City and Western Missouri in Washington—and they are many— few men have served the interests of this immediate territory more diligently and sincerely than have Symington and his able administrative assistant, Stanley Fike. Kansas Citians have found them on the job when anything affecting our area has come up. It is only fair to say so.

That's the way we size this race up.

Coming from the source it did, that editorial expressing the *Kansas City Star*'s feeling concerning him, was about as high an offering of praise as Symington could receive in Missouri.

Somewhat to Symington's consternation, the Republicans nominated a woman, Hazel Palmer, a lawyer from Sedalia, to run for the Senate against him. She was widely known, especially among women's clubs, and he felt uncomfortable with a feminine opponent.

"What if she attacks me?" he asked. "I can't use those tactics against her. I've always treated women just one way— with the courtesy I think a man ought to extend to women."

He was concerned, even, that something he might say or do would be twisted to imply a lack of chivalry to his opponent.

The lady in the case, however, had no such scruples. She was a good speaker, and she went about the state making a vicious and spiteful campaign, calling Symington every name of which she could think, accusing him of every evil motive she could dream up, including "scurrilous labor connections," and appealing to every possible prejudice she could hope to marshal against him.

Symington carefully avoided taking notice of any of her accusations, although he was never so impolite as to ignore the lady herself. This does not, however, mean that he did not campaign hard and earnestly. His instinct for competition is such that he does not know the meaning of complacency, and he would not believe he was sure of victory, even when his friends, after the most careful surveys, assured him he would be an easy victor.

Back and forth across the state he traveled, renewing old friendships, making new ones, discussing his record with any who cared to ask, talking about the state of the Union and the world situation, and sometimes just relaxing to chat about crops or the weather in his simple and friendly manner. At times it hardly seemed he was campaigning at all, so easy did he make it seem. But he *was* campaigning, and at such a rate that once more he left everyone around him exhausted.

Election day came and when the returns were in the results were astounding; not because Symington won, but because so many people turned out to vote for him, on an off year, when it was apparent that he was sure of election anyway.

His majority was 385,000 in round figures, the largest off-year election majority in the history of his state. His percentage of the votes, 67 per cent against 33 per cent for his opponent was the greatest ever run up in a state-wide race in Missouri. Said the *St. Louis Globe-Democrat:*

> The returns show that the junior Senator received not only the full complement of Democratic votes cast but thousands of Republican and independent votes as well.

Symington carried every Congressional district in the state; and by a bigger margin than did the Congressman from the district, except in three instances. This was unheard of in Missouri. Very few Senators ever carry districts by bigger majorities than the local Congressmen.

Symington, for instance, was the first Democratic candidate for state-wide office ever to carry the traditionally Republican southwest Missouri Congressional district. He did that in 1958. Truman never carried that district. Champ Clark, for all his popularity, never carried it. Franklin Delano Roosevelt never carried it.

Once more Stuart Symington had shown an almost magical gift of getting votes. It marked him ever more clearly than before for great things.

2

When the returns were in and the great proportions of the victory were known, Symington received telephone calls and telegrams from all over the United States.

Missourians were jubilant. John R. Hahn, writing in the *St. Louis Globe-Democrat*, said:

> The astonishing size of Senator Stuart Symington's triumph in Tuesday's election makes him a top contender for the Democratic Presidential nomination in 1960 and the campaign for the White House was under way yesterday.
>
> Mark R. Holloran, the Democratic National Committeeman for Missouri, said the significant thing about the Symington triumph is the big jump in popularity and percentage of vote totals in 1958 over 1952.
>
> "I am doing everything I can to win support for Senator Symington for the 1960 Presidential nomination," he said. "Now there can be no suggestion that he is running for two offices. It is in order to look ahead to 1960. We Democrats in Missouri have to face up to the fact that we probably have a President in our midst. And Senator Symington will have to face up to it, too.
>
> "He is ideally suited to be President, both from the standpoint of experience, ability, national stature, and geography. I think it would be wonderful if former President Truman were to place Mr. Symington's name in nomination in 1960—and I think it might happen, too."

That kind of enthusiasm in his home state might be taken for granted, but it is heard from other directions, too.

The *Knoxville Sentinel*, a powerful Tennessee, and therefore a Southern newspaper, had the following interesting estimate of him, by Milton Britten, headed "Democrat's Logical Candidate, Symington Has Everything," published June 27, 1959.

Logic lives only on the fringes of politics. So it may be vain to talk of the Democrats having a "logical" Presidential candidate.

Yet logic would seem to demand that the Democrats take a good hard look at one of their officially unannounced candidates who has, to date, barely made the political popularity polls.

This is Sen. Stuart Symington of Missouri, who appears to have just about everything a political party could make Presidential hay with. Just as significant, he lacks some handicaps that plague his rivals. Consider these items:

1. He's a border state man, identified with neither "Northern liberals," nor "Southern conservatives." If any section hates Symington or his views they aren't vocal enough to be heard here. In contrast, able, articulate Hubert Humphrey of Minnesota is anathema in the South.

2. Symington is personally attractive. Tall (6 feet 2) and athletic of build, he has at 58 a youthful air identified with physical vigor rather than age. The party's current front-runner, John Kennedy of Massachusetts, 18 years Symington's junior, is handicapped by the frequent adjective "boyish."

3. Symington, a Yale man, is considered plenty brainy—but not an "egg-head," the sometime designation that may have contributed to two-time loser Adlai Stevenson's defeats.

4. Symington could challenge the opposition on their own terms in discussing business issues. "Have you ever met a payroll?" Vice President Nixon hasn't. Symington during his business career was at various times president of an electrical manufacturing company, an iron and steel company, a radio corporation, had a good record of getting along with labor.

5. War record? Symington was at 17 a second lieutenant in World War I. A champion of air power, he was named Assistant Secretary of War for Air in 1946, and the next year became the nation's first Secretary of the Air Force.

6. Government experience? Besides his Senate and military service he has served in six top-level Government jobs. Nobody in the field of candidates from either party could match this.

Symington's reputation as a defense expert has been a political handicap to the extent that he's busy now trying to prove he's equally informed and interested in other fields.

But with defense taking up the lion's share of the national budget and playing a life-and-death role in international affairs, the "handicap" could be a major asset.

The nation's next President, remember, will succeed hero-soldier Dwight Eisenhower, whose background in military defense is popularly considered one of his strong points as Chief Executive.

7. Backing? Although he hasn't done well in public polls, a recent poll of Congressional Democrats put Symington out in front of the field. Former President Harry Truman has indicated a partiality for him. He has the backing of some "pros." He got a smattering of support at the last Democratic National convention.

He is a familiar figure to the national television audience, for he was a member of the Senate committee that heard the famous McCarthy case against the Pentagon. Most of the hearings were televised, and Symington often directed sharp interrogations to Senator McCarthy . . .

Logic would seem to indicate increasing attention for Symington. But politics, we concede, has a long history of thumbing its nose at logic.

There have been scores of other comments, some equally friendly, some less so, in newspapers and magazines all over the country. Gould Lincoln, in the *Washington Evening Star* of August 5, 1959, viewed it this way:

Senator Stuart Symington of Missouri is making less candidate "noise" today than other Democratic Senators prominently mentioned for President next year—but that may be more to his interest than otherwise.

There seems no slightest doubt . . . that interest in the Missouri Senator is rising, rather than decreasing. This has been revealed in public opinion polls, polls of political leaders, and private interviews.

Holmes Alexander, reviewing Symington's career and achievements in the *Los Angeles Times*, said in part:

He was an excellent industrial manager who saved a couple of floundering firms during a depression time. He was a superb labor-management relationist in the gloomy days when the Wagner Act was being pressed like a crown of thorns upon the brow of American industry.

It is possible, I think, to construct an objective image of Symington, 1960, from the materials of Symington, 1940. And if there is any analogy between the pre-war depression and the post-war cold war, then we possibly can estimate what sort of a President this man might make if elected next year.

Symington's formula for business management . . . comes down to "order and simplicity." He is not talking in a vacuum, for he illustrates what he means . . .

To Symington '40, the Wagner Labor Act and the new wage hour legislation were not the crack of doom. This astonishing young manager regarded the revolutionary Federal intervention as "a great incentive to scheduling." He felt that the new difficulties of business were a challenge to do business in a better, more efficient manner.

Compulsory bargaining with the unions was difficult, but he saw a silver lining to which most employers were blind. He told this 1940 spring convention of the Society for the Advancement of Management that if the new order "has brought the average employer closer to his employees, that is an advantage . . ."

Well, perhaps we should be cautious about all candidates. Skepticism is a sound political rule, but the young Symington had a proven talent for bringing simplicity out of chaos. And he had that marvelous gift of practical optimism which sees hope where others see only despair.

These are not bad traits for any man who might be President in our time.

As a sort of New Year's gift, marking the end of the year 1958 and the beginning of the year 1959, St. Louis named him "The Man of the Year." He received the honor with pleasure and modesty, as he has other honors, including the Wright Brothers' trophy from the National Aeronautical Association, the General Hap Arnold trophy from the Veterans of Foreign Wars, Aviation's Man of the Year (twice), two United States decorations—the Medal for Merit and the Distinguished Service Medal—and numerous honorary college degrees, together with kudos of various other kinds.

One of the honors that means most to him and touched him deepest was when Hickman Mills, Missouri, which was devastated by a tornado May 20, 1957, named its new grade school for him, in gratitude for his great services in organizing and getting relief and Federal funds for rehabilitation of the stricken area.

In the meantime, Symington returned to Washington, and continued quite imperturbably to conduct his duties as Senator. And to keep his mind at work on new ideas.

XVI

A BID FOR
WORLD DISARMAMENT

1

"The world has now come upon one of those rare moments when all forces converge and hang for a brief instant in the most delicate balance, when civilizations may be made or unmade—almost literally—by the pushing of one button. Our civilization—mature, perhaps a trifle too much at its ease—has entered, together with a young and mortal foe, into a chamber from which neither can emerge quite the same. One or the other may never emerge at all."

It was Stuart Symington, speaking at St. Louis. And it was a prelude to a statement of his feeling that the peace of the world, gravely in danger, must be preserved at any cost, and by every exercise of thought, understanding, and labor for its cause.

Symington has never written off the possibility of an agreement among the nations to reduce their military establishments and devote their energies and research in the nuclear field to producing power and other devices for the good instead of the peril of humanity, some time before it is too late.

To this end, in March 1955, he offered a new disarmament plan in the Senate. Officially it was entitled the Economic

Disarmament Resolution, but it was soon dubbed the "Butter Over Guns" resolution by the press.

In it Symington approached the problem from an angle hitherto unexplored by the Government. His resolution left the standard pattern of disarmament proposals, which customarily suggest numerical or percentage ratios of armed forces or cuts in armed forces.

Rather, it turned to an economic basis for disarmament, with the objective of shifting key resources, such as steel, from military to nonmilitary uses. His thinking was along the line that low living standards are a chief cause of war, and improved living standards for the world's people would promote peace. By devoting larger amounts of basic resources to making good things for the use and betterment and pleasure of the masses, unrest and resentments would at least in a measure be allayed, and good will among the nations extended.

The Symington Resolution embraced seven major points:

1. Through international agreement, the amount of key resources any nation could devote to arms would be limited.

2. Military resource ceilings would be set at levels designed to attain a major increase in living standards for the people of each nation. The ratio of resources for peace could be gradually increased.

3. There would be a foolproof inspection system. Violation would be automatic evidence of aggressive intent.

4. A basis for an all-out moral offensive against arms and for higher living standards would be provided.

5. World attention would be focussed on how each nation apportioned its resources between peaceful and warlike uses.

6. Full pressure of world opinion could be brought to bear

upon Communist leaders to improve the living standards of their people.

7. The President would present the plan to the United Nations for consideration.

Under Symington's plan, emphasis was placed on the vast value that could be obtained by the millions of common people of the world if the billions of dollars spent yearly by their governments for armament were devoted instead to their welfare—the housing, food, clothing, recreation, transportation, and other necessities and pleasures. It was called idealistic by some, but it embraced a basic truth that contains universal appeal, and by so much becomes realistic.

The chronology of events that succeeded the announcement of and introduction of the Symington Resolution is interesting:

March 1, 1955—Senator Symington released a statement explaining the nature and purpose of a disarmament resolution he planned to introduce in the Senate.

March 2—Senator Symington introduced the resolution and requested that it be left on the table until March 7, for co-sponsors. So highly important was his proposal regarded that forty-seven other Senators joined in co-sponsoring the Symington Resolution.

March 7—Senator Symington's resolution was made the subject of a full-scale criticism on the Moscow radio. Among other things the Russian spokesmen referred to the proposal as "ridiculous," but the attention paid to it was an indication of the importance with which the Soviet leaders treated it.

March 8—In a speech on the Senate floor, Senator Symington explained his resolution in detail.

March 10—President Eisenhower was asked in his press conference what he thought of Senator Symington's resolution, and he replied: "I find here recently more and more occasions to refer to my favorite author. I think you might find the same idea in a speech I delivered, I believe, on April 16, 1953. . . ."

March 19—President Eisenhower created the post of Special Assistant on Disarmament.

June 7—Senator Symington testified before the Senate Foreign Relations Committee in support of his resolution.

The Foreign Relations Committee sent it to the Department of State, with a request for an evaluation.

Back, after an appreciable time lapse, came the following opinion from the State Department:

> The Department of State is in full accord with the underlying objective of reducing armaments with a view to improving living standards [but] it is of particular importance in any disarmament program that provisions for internal control of atomic energy and nuclear weapons be included.

"Nuclear weapons," of course, had not been spelled out in the resolution, any more than had "planes" or "navies" or "guns," but they were all implicit under the general term "arms."

The Department of State also said "any disarmament resolution should allow the discretion of the President in determining the precise nature and timing of further United States proposals to the United Nations on the question of disarmament."

In other words, it would never do for a move toward disarmament to originate in the Senate, where the Administration could not take credit for it.

July 18—The Department of State's substitute plan was offered to the Big Four nations, by Eisenhower, four and a half months after Symington offered his resolution, and seven weeks after the Senate Foreign Relations Committee sent it to the Department of State for "evaluation."

The Eisenhower proposal was for limitation of armaments, including nuclear weapons, with international controls and inspections, including exchanges of blueprints of military establishments, and mutual aerial reconnaissance, the so-called Open Skies policy. This was an elaboration of, but contained nothing not included in, the Symington resolution. The inspection system was as near "foolproof"—the Symington stipulation—as anyone could devise at the time. It was promptly rejected by Russia on the point of the international controls and inspections, especially the aerial reconnaissance. A counterproposal was made by Russia for reduction of armed forces on a basis not acceptable to the United States.

July 25—The Senate passed a resolution calling for the creation of a Disarmament Subcommittee. In recognition of his pioneering on this line Senator Symington was named a member of this committee, and his resolution was later made a part of the committee's special publications, under the title *Disarmament and Security*.

July 28—The Senate of the United States unanimously passed Senator Symington's Economic Disarmament Resolution, as Senate Resolution 71.

2

It is important to remember that Symington's proposal did not request that the United States and Russia alone should be involved in the disarmament program, but rather asked the President of the United States to present the proposal to the United Nations for further explanation and study. It also requested the President to direct appropriate government agencies to undertake new studies which would assist in reaching the objectives of the resolution.

Unfortunately the economic aspect of the resolution which might have had so much appeal was not stressed in the State Department negotiations that followed. The rulers of Russia, quite evidently, did not want their people to know that such an idea was in the wind. It might have created complications behind the Iron Curtain.

"While it is not accurate to say that Senator Symington's resolution was the sole force which stimulated subsequent proposals and actions in the field of disarmament," says Dr. E. C. Welsh, "it can accurately be said that it had some catalytic influence both on the Executive branch and in the Congress. It would seem to be more than mere coincidence that the establishment of a Special Assistant to the President on Disarmament, and the creation of a Disarmament Subcommittee in the Senate, should have followed so closely the Senator's disarmament proposal."

The history of disarmament efforts since then is well known. The following year the United Nations again brought forward the subject, urging disarmament and nuclear controls along substantially the same lines pioneered by the Symington resolution. Again Russia said "Nyet," particularly to the internal inspections and aerial photography.

Then, surprisingly, Russia announced in March 1957 that it had unilaterally suspended testing of nuclear weapons, and proposed the United States do likewise. The proposal caught the Administration napping, and placed it severely on the defensive, while it was torn at its highest levels by arguments over the advisability of discontinuing the tests.

Embarrassed, the State Department said that the United States had "discussed" seizing that advantage itself, by announcing its willingness to "negotiate suspension"—after the tests it was about to begin in the Marshall Islands.

But Harold Macmillan, Prime Minister of Britain, suggested a summit meeting to be held in the United Nations Security Council. To this Khrushchev at first agreed, then changed his mind.

Now the United States came up with a suggestion of its own: that all three nations should jointly explore the problem of whether nuclear blasts could be detected.

On August 21, almost six months after the Soviet announcement of suspension of nuclear tests, scientists said that detection could be "technically feasible," provided a net of detection stations was established. At this Eisenhower announced that, beginning October 31, this country would suspend its tests for a year, provided the U. S. S. R. did not resume testing.

But the Soviets, after having discontinued tests for half a year, resumed them again in September.

Again at a loss, the Administration, when the October 31 deadline passed, decided not to resume its tests for the present.

Later the Russian tests also were discontinued, and an uneasy truce in that respect existed.

All of this created concern and impatience in Symington, who hates to see his Government outmaneuvered, with Russia apparently calling the turns.

"Is there," he exclaimed, "in all honesty, any real Administration program? One is reminded of bubble gum. You chew on it awhile—you blow it up big—and then it bursts. Then you start all over again, perhaps with a different flavor.

"That's fine for children and bubble gum; but how is it for a nation's international policy and program?"

3

The problem is still before the nations and the world.

And Symington believes deeply that no effort should be spared to bring to a successful consummation some plan of disarmament.

"Peace is no longer a vacuum between two wars," he said. "It must be waged to be won."

The two giant powers of the world today are Russia and its satellite countries on the one hand, and the United States and its allies on the other.

That makes Russia, to Symington's mind, second in importance only to his own country as a matter for study, and he has made himself one of the best informed men in all America today on the Soviet thinking, philosophies, pattern of behavior, internal problems, resources, ethnic variations, goals, and other important details. His wide information has been obtained by hard and continuous study, using every available source of authoritative information, including intelligence reports, Governmental discussions on every level, interviews with persons who can speak from personal knowledge on various facets of the subject; even the careful reading of Moscow propaganda and the lengthy speeches of various Red leaders, from Khrushchev on down, with a view of trying to understand what is behind those utterances.

His interest and concern in this matter goes a long way back. To illustrate: when his two sons, Stuart and Jim, returned from service in the Army and Marines respectively at the end of World War II, he talked to them about continuing their education which had been interrupted by military service. Both young men wished to be lawyers, which greatly pleased him, since it not only was a continuation of the profession his father had practiced, but had once been his own youthful ambition.

But when they went off to school, he urged them strongly to study the Russian language as one of their elective courses, and inform themselves thoroughly on Russia in general.

Both sons are now competent Russian linguists, and the accomplishment has been of value in numerous ways. For example, not long ago a Russian who was interested in science, was entertained by Jim Symington, and was delighted to find that he could converse in his own tongue with his American host. That particular Russian returned to his own country with a heightened respect and liking for America in general; which if it could be multiplied many times over might lead to a better understanding between the nations, at least among the common people.

The leaders of the U. S. S. R., of course, are a different matter.

As Symington warned in May 1955, "The leaders of Russia have not only constantly reiterated their goal of world dominion, they have also predicted the doom of all other political systems, particularly Capitalism. They have inflamed all Communists against non-Communists wherever the latter may be. They have sealed off their own people behind the Iron Curtain, while taking advantage of free access in other countries to create constant distress and confusion within."

And how do they do it?

Because they have perhaps the best-trained as well as the largest corps of foreign operatives and diplomatic agents in the world, he points out.

Once Britain had the finest corps of career diplomats and foreign service experts in the world. But Russia has shown spectacular abilities to get to the people of other nations, often in a manner that left the Free World gasping.

In Arab countries, Russian agents mingle with the people, live with them, speak their dialects and foist their ideas upon them from the lowliest peasants to the palaces of the rulers. In India, the British found Russian agents excelling their own famed experts in acting and speaking like the natives until they seemed to belong to them, meanwhile constantly breeding dissension and rebellion. Russian agents in China speak the many tongues of China, and know Chinese manners, customs, and protocol. In Latin America, Malaya, Africa, or, when it comes down to it, in Germany, Italy, France, Great Britain or the United States, agents from Russia can hardly be separated from the populations of those countries.

Foreign languages are compulsory in Russian elementary and secondary schools. Superior students go to the National Institute of Foreign Languages to be perfected in the languages they specialize in, while the Institute of Foreign Relations, supervised by the Russian Ministry of Foreign Affairs, is turning out around 1,000 trained, indoctrinated, highly adroit foreign service people every year.

"The Russians are developing the most linguistically proficient diplomatic corps in the world, whereas our representatives live in isolation, associating mostly with other Americans, because they lack the training and do not understand the language and culture of the country to which they are sent," Symington says.

Since it is all a part of the world-wide problem, he introduced, January 9, 1959, a bill to establish a United States Foreign Service Academy on an equal rating with West Point, Annapolis, and the Air Force Academy, "to train young people for efficient service in diplomatic missions thoughout the world."

In a magazine article he wrote about his proposal, Symington said:

Fifty per cent of our entire Foreign Service diplomatic corps does not have a speaking knowledge of *any* foreign language. Seventy-five per cent of the new men coming into Foreign Service do not speak a foreign language. There is only *one* United States Ambassador to any Communist country who speaks the language of the country to which he is assigned, and that is Llewellyn E. Thompson, United States Ambassador to Moscow.

The proposed academy would charge no tuition, applicants would have to pass a competitive examination and be selected on a basis of merit, a fair percentage of young women would be allowed to enroll, and though the academy would be under the direction of the Secretary of State, it would train people to serve in any Government agency overseas.

"The ultimate future of the world, whether it is to be free or slave, will not be settled on the battlefields, but rather in the minds of men," Symington says. And he adds:

"Every Communist revolutionary sent out to infiltrate, divide, and conquer, ought to be matched by a Free World advocate of 'lasting peace through justice and law'—someone as energetic and effective as his opposite number from behind the Iron Curtain."

Too often, he believes, we send out representatives who are unskilled and often bungling amateurs, expecting them to compete with highly trained and expert professionals in attempting to handle sensitive relations between the nations. It is one of the grave weaknesses of our system.

"Tomorrow is too late," he says. "We ought to be starting

today training our representatives to merchandise the most valuable commodity in the world—the American way of life, with its individual dignity and its investment in freedom."

4

As to the present world situation, Symington is not an alarmist, though he feels very strongly that peace will not be maintained by talk, but instead by strength.

"You can't negotiate from weakness," is one of his sayings. "You have to have the power to enforce peace, and the enemy must know you have it, and then you can talk to him on even terms."

He has been gravely concerned over the internal squabblings of the NATO nations, some of it due to Russian pressure, and he continually studies foreign leaders—Khrushchev, De Gaulle, Adenauer, Macmillan, and the rest.

Some time ago he foresaw an era of trouble in our own hemisphere, and predicted it. Now that it is here, in the Carribean and some South American countries, he thinks it will require more of our attention, may distract some of our effort from global interest and responsibilities.

Some of this, again, is due to Communist infiltration and breeding of dissension, he feels.

The Soviet method is always to attack, he points out. Barefacedly false charges are made against the United States and "other Capitalistic countries." When Red armies move into Laos, there are trumpetings that "warmongering" America is to blame. Khrushchev broadcasts a promise to "bury" the Free World. The Russians promise anything, especially in areas where human poverty and misery exist, with a cynical knowledge that they will not make good on many of those promises.

Every move toward disarmament is vetoed with abusive speeches. And all of this keeps unrest and apprehension stirring in the world.

For what purpose? To carry out the Communist program to dominate the world, by political means short of war is possible, but by force if necessary.

Yet he does not foresee war in the immediate future.

"Why should the Russians risk war when they're getting everything they want without it?" he asks. "More than forty years ago, at the Treaty of Brest-Litovsk, the Russians gave up about everything of value they had, except a couple of cities—Leningrad and Moscow—to buy time. Today they control a third of the earth's surface and half the population of the world. And most of this has been done by infiltration, indoctrination, undermining, and taking over."

So long as America stays strong, Communism will not achieve its object of overrunning the globe, he believes. But it already has extended far too widely for the security and interests of the Free World, and some day this Nation may find itself where it must say, "This far, and no farther."

XVII

STRENGTH: THE ROAD TO PEACE

1

So often has Symington spoken in public and private on the threat to our national security, that persons less concerned over it, or less farseeing, have sometimes said he was "overemphasizing" it. But he passionately believes that it cannot be overemphasized, and that the people must be made to understand the great peril that hangs over them continually.

And in this connection his one great objective, his real concern, is the attainment of a just and lasting peace. Over and over he has stressed that fundamental. Only by strength can this Nation survive. Weakness invites, almost assures, destruction.

Yet to achieve and maintain this position of strength, the thundercloud of danger must be understood. In a recent issue of *Missiles and Rockets* magazine, he wrote:

> There are many experts on past wars, but none on future wars. As Gen. Maxwell D. Taylor, Chief of Staff of the U.S. Army testified: "In my judgment, any dogmatic prediction of what will take place after an initial exchange is beyond human capability."
>
> Let us hope there will never be any real experts on nuclear wars, not on the grounds that no one would survive to become

an expert, but on the premise that we may have the courage and wisdom to prevent such destruction from ever getting started.

It is not enough, however, for us to be comforted by such a hope. We must also be prepared for the dreadful alternative. In fact, such preparedness may well be the only sound basis upon which a hope for peace will grow.

If nuclear war does happen, it will come with such suddenness and destruction that there will be no time to defend or retaliate with any strength except that already in existence. Neither weapons on the drawing boards nor those whose production was postponed will have any effect on the outcome of the conflict.

Since the time factor for response to an attack may be but a matter of minutes, the state of readiness of our weapons is of crucial importance. Those forces not so alert may be no asset; in fact, they may turn out to have been an actual handicap as a pre-attack source of unwarranted complacency.

For almost two decades, Stuart Symington has had an active role in the defense of his country. Not only as a student of defense, but as a man of action he has made significant contributions to America's defense thinking and America's defense strength.

His experience is unparalleled. No one else in Congress, or in the Executive branch, has had as varied a range of contacts with defense issues as has Symington. While in private business, he produced military equipment for the armed forces in World War II. He lived through the German bomb and missile blitzes of London and Liverpool. He has administered, as a policy-level Government official, large elements of our defense establishment. As the first Secretary of the Air Force, he organized that new service, and he played an important part in forming the Defense Department reorganization, and defended that program before Congress.

He administered the disposal of surplus military property; was in charge of gaining a stockpile of scarce strategic materials; and as a member of the National Security Council, the highest defense policy group in the Nation, participated in the formulation of defense plans and policies. He administered both lending and tax programs for accelerating the expansion of essential facilities in private industry. As a member of the Senate, he sponsored legislation, conducted investigations, and informed the public regarding the Nation's defense problems.

Out of his wealth of constructive experience, Stuart Symington has developed a clear and consistent philosophy about our national defense.

Since his days as Secretary of the Air Force, he has been witnessing what he calls "the deterioration of our relative position in strike capability." This he charges to Administration policy, not to lack of United States economic strength.

"Economically America is much stronger today than the U. S. S. R.," he says. "With millions less people, we produce more than twice as much as the Soviet does. It is true that their rate of progress, as well as that of China, is rapid. But it is also true that we can far out-produce the Soviets in weaponry, with less drain and less strain.

"Knowledge that we have this production potential, however, is not enough. We must use it. There is no time left for complacency. Rather, we should look with clear vision at realities."

Consistently, both as Secretary of the Air Force and as Senator, he has fought for greater efficiency in the armed services, and he considers the Pentagon, in its present state, very inefficient.

"It is as if the three armed services were each preparing to fight the next war alone, without any cooperation from their fellow services," he says.

He believes with all his heart in greater unification of the armed forces, and was a prime mover and active exponent of the unification legislation passed in 1958 and previously. But during debates and after passage he asserted time and again that though it was a step in the right direction, it still did not go far enough toward unification.

The present huge, unwieldly, red-tape-wrapped Pentagon organization, he feels, is like a morass through which it is far too difficult for constructive new ideas to pass, and which in addition is a tremendous waste of the taxpayers' money.

"There should be just one chain of command, with centralized buying, and centralized research," he insists. And he adds that lack of real unification in the services, with interservice jealousies and interservice duplications has at least two major evil effects: it weakens our defense position, and it unnecessarily burdens the people of the Nation with expenditures for which they do not get a defense return.

"We have," he says, "two armies and six air forces, not to mention the divergent branches of our naval establishment, with all the waste and inefficiency such multiplicity creates. Service rivalries and the resulting efforts of each service to build up its own prestige and its own inventory of weapons at the expense of other services, is costly in time, effort, money, and in defense effectiveness."

His ideas as to what should be done are clear-cut:

Instead of the present archaic setup, the Pentagon should be reorganized on the principle of "function or mission to be performed." All elements of all services with strategic capabilities should be in one joint command. This is not true now.

In the Air Force hearings General LeMay, then commander of the Strategic Air Command, said:

"We never are able to plan definitely on the fleet because we don't know where they are going to be. It all depends on how the war starts and what they have decided to do."

The Navy perhaps feels the same way about the Air Force, and of course it would act as efficiently and quickly as possible. But the point is that there is no central command over the two forces. One could very well be operating in one direction while the other went in a different way.

In addition to unifying strategic commands of all branches, Symington believes all elements for continental defense should be drawn into another joint command. A third joint command should handle small or limited war responsibilities, and a fourth should be in charge of the supporting and "house-keeping" functions of all.

These, of course, would be under a supreme command, responsible for their proper use, including the over-all planning in case of real or anticipated war, subject always to the authority of the President as Commander-in-Chief.

It is pretty certain that changes such as these would create a howl in certain quarters. Generals are generals, and admirals are admirals, and gold braid will always want to keep all its prerogatives and privileges as at present constituted. Yet there is more than a fair number of the thinking military people who agree with Symington, and would like to see a greater system of command efficiency established.

Characteristically, the Senator puts it in terms of balance sheets:

"If we had a reorganization like that, accompanied by a real over-all weapons systems evaluation to eliminate duplications and obsolescent weapons, we could save the taxpayers tens of millions of dollars *every week*. Or, by putting the money saved by the elimination of the present waste back into defense, we could vastly increase our position over what it is now."

In a speech in the Senate, August 30, 1957, he said:

"We are properly indignant because a young warrant officer in a far northern outpost caused the waste of $33,000 worth of surplus equipment. But we are comfortably complacent about the fact that, in effect, the present Administration is directing the management of the Department of Defense to throw away $33,000 every three minutes, 24 hours a day, 365 days a year; through waste . . . alone.

"If this enormous waste caused us no sacrifice of national security it would still be outrageous. As it is, the manner in which our defense superiority has been dribbled away is nothing short of tragic; and we have no savings to show for it."

2

Above everything else, Symington insists that the Nation must have an adequate defense. He hopes that the efficiencies he has consistently recommended will some day be instituted, but meantime he has frequently recommended additional money for specific purposes where the facts clearly supported the need.

"Some have questioned our ability to attain adequate military strength," he says. "Of *course* we can afford whatever is necessary for survival! What would be the use of being the richest man in the graveyard?"

On another occasion he put it in a different way:

"A catch phrase often used is: 'We now have the largest peace-time force in our history.'

"What safety would there be in having twice as large a peace-time force as any in our history—if that force could not effectively meet and beat the Communist threat?

"Strength is relative. In other words, in a ball game is it better to have three runs when your opponents have two, or six when your opponents have seven? Relative strength is all that counts. Anything else has exactly the value of the second best poker hand."

This is no broadside approach, which merely says the defense budget should be so much bigger, or so much smaller. Repeatedly, Symington has gone through the labor of intensive factual briefing before he arrived at any conclusion as to strengths or deficiencies in weapons or other aspects of our defense.

Once he reaches the best conclusion, he puts everything into trying to get appropriations for speeding up or augmenting the production of whatever is necessary for maximum safety.

For example, he was the spearhead in pushing for more funds for the heavy bomber force and for the jet tankers to extend the range and support that force. More recently he fought just as hard for a program that would prevent the Communists from increasing their ICBM advantage. And he is now working for the modernization of our relatively small Army.

On the other hand, after fully informing himself, he has also pointed out the obsolescence of certain expensive weapons systems, such as the Nike and Bomarc antiaircraft missiles, and sought for greater emphasis on antisubmarine warfare by the Navy, instead of the very expensive aircraft carriers.

Symington is interested in all aspects of the armed services, not just in the strengthening of the Air Force.

3

Historically, after World War II, the United States cut back more than it should have in both research and readiness. Symington opposed it at the time.

Yet, even after these cutbacks the Nation remained by far the most powerful country in the world. America, and only America, had the atomic weapons and the heavy bombers to deliver them.

But policy continued to favor further cutbacks. When, in the pre-Korea economy drive the Air Force was reduced to forty-eight wings, Symington resigned in silent protest from his post as Secretary of the Air Force. In the Korean War that followed, his judgment in opposing reduction of the Nation's air power was sharply vindicated.

With billions being spent for ICBM armament the question has been raised as to whether this great country can afford to do more. Symington's categorical answer is that we cannot afford *not* to do more.

He points out that under present policies the Department of Defense military expenditures are steadily decreasing in the percentage of the national budget devoted to them, and also represent a smaller percentage of the national production of wealth.

"The Department of Defense is spending about 63 cents per capita per day," Symington said not long ago. "If five cents, or the cost of one pack of chewing gum, were added to this per capita per day figure, it would add up to about $3.2 billion a year. An addition like that would enable us to more than double the program for ICBM's and go far toward real modernization of our Army."

This does not mean necessarily, he points out, that defense expenditures ceilings should be raised by $3.2 billion. He goes back to the many actions which could be taken to save prodigious sums in the Department of Defense.

Symington recognizes that one of the great characteristics of the atomic age in which we live is the importance of what is called "lead time." Decisions must be made today, in order for results to occur five years from today. You cannot build an aircraft carrier, train a scientist, get a college education, or defend a continent on twenty-four hours' notice. Each has its own time span and you either make the decision in advance or face the consequences later on.

In this connection, on one phase of defense he is very emphatic: the significance of the missile gap cannot be overestimated, and confusion about the understanding of that gap is due not so much to intelligence estimates, as to varying degrees of willingness to face the facts. The importance of telling the people the truth is a thing he stresses over and over, and he points out that regardless of exact figures or exact ratios, it is admitted by everyone who has any real knowledge of the subject that the ICBM gap is widening, and our present program, for fiscal reasons, is geared to let that gap continue to widen.

4

Senator Symington's thinking on national defense is definite and at the same time broad. Its major points can be summed up as follows:

1. Our national defense is not a toy to be played with and discarded from time to time for political, fiscal, or emotional reasons. Rather, it is a twenty-four-hour-day essential, "like

oxygen," which must be maintained if we are to keep the freedoms of democracy which we so highly prize.

2. This great country can afford the money and effort needed to defend our way of life. Conversely, we cannot afford to spend less.

3. To maintain this defense does not necessarily mean more expenditures of the taxpayers' money, but it does mean more defense for each tax dollar spent. We are now, and we have been for some time, receiving an inexcusably small defense return for our investment in weapons, personnel and organization.

4. To obtain this greater defense return for each dollar it is essential that the Defense Department and its various components be reorganized in accordance with the realities of this nuclear-space age. It will require major changes, since the organization and many of the plans now developed, are geared to fighting past wars, rather than for deterring or, if necessary, fighting a future war.

5. The most practical program to modernize the defense structure includes reorganization of the separate military services into unified commands, for such specific missions as strategic retaliation, continental defense, limited wars, and logistical support for the other commands. There also must be a thorough evaluation of all weapons systems to eliminate duplication and obsolescence on one hand, and accelerate and expand the operational readiness of those needed and worthwhile. With this must go a thorough revision of the military personnel system, to develop and maintain a trained, dedicated military force. Increased attention must be devoted to the research and development of new systems, while at the same time maintaining a strong existing posture.

6. Since the time factor for response to an attack may be but a matter of minutes, the state of readiness of our weapons systems and manpower is of crucial importance. "We cannot retaliate with blueprints or good intentions, or even an embossed statement showing a balanced budget."

7. It is dangerous to measure our retaliatory strength in terms of what we have as compared to what the possible enemy has, prior to their attack on us. Our strength must be judged on what we believe we would have left, *after* an attack.

8. A strong strategic striking force, composed of aircraft as well as land and submarine based missiles, is essential as a deterrent against all-out war and as an umbrella under which —but not with which—we can meet our commitments in case of small wars.

9. Not only must we have such strength and keep it modern and alert, but we must also have mobile (by air) ground forces, with the most modern equipment possible, for fighting such limited wars. Such forces will also act as a deterrent against aggression of Communist powers against small nations of the Free World.

10. The basic objective of a strong defense position is world peace, with freedom and respect for the individual. "Ostrichlike thinking" of those who would "wish our troubles away" is just as dangerous as the "saber rattling" of those who boast through ignorance. We can achieve world peace only if we are ready to negotiate from a position of strength rather than a position of weakness.

11. Not only must we have a strong defense, but the possible enemy must know we have it, and everyone must know that we are determined to use that strength if we must.

12. Above all, the American people must be given all the facts about our defense, except for such information as might

assist a possible enemy. "If the people have the facts, both as to the relative strengths and the dangers, they will support every expenditure and every sacrifice that is necessary."

That is Stuart Symington speaking on the great issue of national defense.

XVIII

LEVELHEADED LIBERAL

1

The liberals of the great depression were pump primers. The Nation was suffering from a contracted money supply, over-concentration of wealth, lack of purchasing power at the base. All sorts of expedients were resorted to, some of them jeered at as boon-doggling—by persons who did not happen to be face-to-face with the necessity of selling apples on the street corners to keep from starving.

Out of the depression grew guarantees for labor, unemployment insurance, social security, the principle of Government *investment*, and other measures which at the time were opposed by the conservatives, but which now are generally accepted as having proved advantageous.

Today, with employment in nearly satisfactory condition, liberalism has taken on a new form, and Symington represents the new type of liberal.

He believes, for example, that our new form of capitalism has greater potential than the old "law of the jungle" capitalism, which David Ricardo described.

"The greatest thing we've discovered is purchasing power *at the base*," he says. "True prosperity arises from strong and steady purchasing power at the base, instead of spasmodic trickles from the full tubs and buckets of the financially better off.

"Business is healthier when workers live like human beings, and buy homes, and automobiles, and a few luxuries. That's the new concept. That's why the United States is of all countries the most wonderfully adapted to the world of today.

"The old concept was different. I remember as a young man working in a company when a new owner of the 'old school' took over. He looked out on the parking lot where a few broken-down jalopies were parked, and asked, 'Who do those cars belong to?' He was told they belonged to his workers. 'You're paying them too much if they can afford cars,' he said. 'Cut their wages.' He didn't realize that when men like his employees were making enough to afford a little in convenience and luxury it was helping him, helping all business."

Very strongly Symington holds that in the new capitalism private and public initiative must work hand-in-hand.

"There's a big difference between public *spending* of the 'pump-priming' type," he points out, "and public *investment*, such as the building of highways, schools, hospitals, nursing homes for the aged, river development, reforestation, and conservation of natural resources. Public investment generates new wealth, new jobs, and is as important as private investment. Yet some of the men who are strongest against it are the very ones who boast about spending stockholder dollars for the erection of new plants and the installation of new facilities in their own businesses. It works the same way in either case."

As to the Nation's economy, which he considers as important as the Nation's defense, he believes that adequate Government leadership is most important in keeping it healthy.

"One thing is certain," he told an audience at Clarksburg, West Virginia, March 7, 1959, "a depression is not the fault of the people who suffer from it. Depressions are comparable with earthquakes—they are caused by deep-seated faults and shifts in the underlying structure of the country.

"Like earthquakes, tornadoes or floods, they are beyond the power of any single individual to prevent. But there is one difference. The people, acting together through their Government, can prevent depressions.

"Use of food and fiber surpluses to relieve distress, retooling of depressed areas to increase income and employment, training of workers replaced by machines for new jobs, improvement of roads and airports to aid the flow of commerce and industry, Government action to bring men and jobs together, are only a few of the many steps that can be taken by intelligent Government leadership."

2

"For a number of years," Symington says, "there has been increasing disagreement among certain segments of our economy—especially management, labor, and capital—on some of the most important problems incident to our growth and prosperity. There is disagreement on taxation, interest rates, hours of work, automation, the causes of inflation, and just how far the Government should go into the management of our economy.

"Now, differences of opinion are all right. But these are not mere differences of opinion. These are hardening into battle lines. Like soldiers at the front, each group has stockpiled economic arguments to support its own position; and they spend a good deal of effort lobbing propaganda shells into the trenches of the 'enemy,' each blaming the others for inflation, for recession, and for other economic woes.

"Ninety-nine-plus percent of the members of these various segments of our economy are good Americans who cherish freedom and our way of life. I believe there is a much wider area of agreement among them than some of them would appear to admit. Why shouldn't these domestic differences be ironed out, face to face?"

His recommendation is as follows:

The Administration should sponsor "summit meetings" of banking, business, and labor leaders to consider domestic affairs.

"They do it for international affairs, don't they?" he asked. "Why not for national affairs? Real leadership could reconcile most of the differences, find ways to curb inflation, and persuade capital, management and labor to pull together for the good of America."

The nation-wide steel strike that began July 15, 1959, furnished an example of lack of Administration leadership, he charges. Several weeks before the strike began he urged the President to act. He did so again just prior to the strike. And on August 4 he introduced a Concurrent Resolution in the Senate, in which thirty-one other Senators joined him as co-sponsors, calling for action by the President looking to a settlement of the strike.

He was not talking from mere theory when he made the proposal, for he had illustrated rather vividly by personal actions what kind of good could be obtained by bringing the leaders of divergent elements together.

A typical episode occurred while he was Secretary of the Air Force. The Bendix Corporation was then producing parts for the B-36 bomber, at that time the one real deterrent to

Soviet aggression, and it became involved in a strike. As the strike continued, Air Force officers told Symington that the B-36 was getting into trouble. Shortly thereafter the Chief of Staff notified him that unless spare parts came out of Bendix in two weeks at most, the B-36's would be grounded.

Symington's ensuing moves were prompt, purposeful—and resultful.

He first called Walter Reuther, president of the United Automobile Workers, and asked him to come to his office next day. Reuther agreed.

He then telephoned M. P. Ferguson, head of the Bendix plant, who at first said that under no conditions did he want to negotiate with Reuther.

Symington emphasized that he did not want to get into the collective bargaining process, but he felt it important for the head of the company and the head of the union to realize the danger to America if the strike continued. When Ferguson still demurred, Symington told him that unless he came it would become a matter of public record, and it would be necessary for him to be very critical of the company.

Ferguson agreed to come, and he and Reuther met Symington in his office in the Pentagon next morning at about ten o'clock.

"They talked before lunch, during lunch, and throughout the afternoon," Symington recalls. "At the end of the day I went in to the meeting and told them I was going home, that the cafeteria was going to stay open all night, and that I only asked they did not leave my office until they had reached a settlement, this in the interest of national security.

"Next morning when I came to work around eight-thirty o'clock, they were still there, having negotiated through the night. In the forenoon of that day, after being at it for more than twenty-four hours without intermission, they signed the contract.

"To me one of the best parts about this story was that some time later, when I saw Mr. Ferguson, he volunteered that he had been wrong in first opposing the meeting. 'Because,' he said, 'we signed a good contract and since then we have had no labor trouble whatever.'"

"It was experiences like this, and I've had several of them in the past, which made me so anxious to have the President point out to both the industry and the steelworkers the grave danger which would result from an extended steel strike."

There was no action from the White House in response to the Senate resolution, and the steel strike became the longest in history without any Government action before the Taft-Hartley law was finally invoked on October 9, 1959. This was not the way Symington believed the crippling strike should have been handled. At the very beginning, the union leaders should have been brought into contact with the steel executives who had power to act. Under such conditions, Symington believes the strike could have been shortened by many weeks, if not altogether averted.

"When Allen Dulles said this country would be 'virtually committing economic suicide' unless the increase in its gross national product averaged more than 2 percent annually to take care of the net addition in population, he made a statement which should have given apprehension to every American because in recent years our economy has not averaged anything like that percentage," Symington says. "No longer can we consider an extended strike in an industry which is the base of any industrial complex, as purely a domestic matter. Our Government should consider such a loss in our productivity—and this is a loss which can never be regained—from the

standpoint of its effect on our position and that of the Free
World as against the growing strength of the Sino-Soviet
conspiracy."

3

Symington has never been a farmer in the literal sense, although he and a brother did raise cattle for a number of years.

But he has a real personal knowledge of what backbreaking
toil means, the feel of sweat running down his back and
smarting in his eyes, and how hard work develops calluses on
the hands and aches in the muscles. And he has, in his seven
years in the Senate, studied the farm problem as closely and
sympathetically as anyone in Congress.

He has been strongly critical of the policies of Ezra Taft
Benson, Secretary of Agriculture, on three major points:

1. Benson "talks economy but performs oppositely," has
skyrocketed the taxpayers' investment in Government-held
surpluses to $10 billion, yet has *not* improved the economic
position of the farmer.

2. The Department of Agriculture under Benson's regime
has become "The Department For Everybody Else *But* the
Farmer," is inefficient, and the price support program alone
is 954 per cent more costly to *administer* than when Benson
took over.

3. Benson has "cut the heart" out of the parity price support program by gratuitously granting price support to corn
producers with no restrictions on plantings, thereby encouraging farmers to produce still more corn for already bulging
Government stockpiles.

Symington has stood up and fought for the farmers, as
when he said in a speech widely and favorably quoted, which
he delivered at Sioux Falls, South Dakota:

"Loose talk about the farmer being the only beneficiary of Government support is always incorrect, and often hypocritical; and it is particularly unfortunate that so much of this talk comes from the very people who are supposed to be working in the farmer's interest.

"Many other segments of the American economy are heavily supported by the Federal Government. I do not necessarily question the wisdom of these [Federal] allowances, especially if they are incident to a build-up in our national defense structure. But aren't they also a support?

"And how about the minimum wage law? I am for the law. It increases the personal dignity of human beings. It also increases purchasing power at the base, perhaps the greatest single advantage America has over all other countries. But surely a Federal law stipulating that anyone working in interstate commerce must be paid at least one dollar an hour is a support."

As a member of the Senate Committee on Agriculture, his sharp differences with Benson have almost assumed the proportions of a feud.

"I am convinced that as a matter of principle he [Benson] does not believe the Government has a right to help farmers or other people when disaster forces them to their knees," he stated at Oklahoma City some time ago.

"The only major farm program advanced by the Republican Administration," he says, "has been flexible or sliding price supports."

And, "faced by 'fixed costs,' under sliding prices this program works to aggravate rather than improve the surplus situation. Whoever is benefitting from this muddling in the farmer's welfare, it is clear that it is neither the farmer nor the consumer.

"The facts are that the cost of what the farmer buys has gone up and stayed up, while the value of what he receives for what he produces has gone down and stayed down."

He puts his finger unerringly on the weakness of the Benson farm policy, which to say the best for it, is based on apparent ignorance of human nature, human instinct, and human motives on the part of the farmers.

"The basis of the Benson farm policy," he says, "is that lower farm prices will discourage production. In other words, if price supports were lowered, farmers would produce less; and that would bring supply in line with demand.

"But most farmers, unwilling tools of this experiment, quickly saw the flaw in the theory. They knew that if the price per bushel or pound went down, more bushels or more pounds would be needed to obtain enough dollars to meet fixed costs, let alone maintain a reasonable standard of living."

The problem of agriculture is complicated, he readily agrees. But it is more a matter of good management than anything else, something it is not now enjoying.

The Benson bureaucracy has especially drawn his fire.

"Since the Department of Agriculture was created in 1889," he says, "there have been fourteen Secretaries of Agriculture —plus Benson. If Mr. Benson continues to operate at the present rate, by the end of the next fiscal year he will have spent more money than all of his fourteen predecessors combined.

"Let his own figures speak for themselves: This Administration has raised the cost of *administering* the price support program from $34 million in 1952, to $364 million in 1958— an increase of 954 per cent. It has added to the payroll 22,000 employees. And what worries me is the growing realization that these people simply do not know where they are going. In

1952 the Commodity Credit Corporation owned some $1 billion of farm commodities. According to the President's budget message, its total investment by June 1960 was to be $10 billion.

"They plant their propaganda in city newspapers and weekly magazines favorable to their cause, and if they were half as successful helping farmers as they are criticizing the farmers, we would have a far better farm program today.

"One of the stories these bureaucrats try to sell is that the farm problem is the result of the inefficiency of the farmers. That is just not true. American farmers are the most efficient and productive in the world.

"Here are a few figures. Last year, average per acre yields on nearly every major commodity set new records. We now produce the same amount of food and fiber on 57 acres that in 1940 we produced in 100 acres. This nation produces more pounds of meat with less feed than ever before. Since 1944, milk production per cow has increased 39 per cent. And all this has only been done by hard work—twelve, fourteen, sometimes sixteen hours a day."

Symington has proposed that the American farmer has a right to receive a fair price for his farm products, assistance in cooperative efforts to adjust production levels to demand, increased distribution of surplus farm products both at home and abroad and emphasis placed on foreign trade, improved drought assistance, adequate conservative measures, and proper crop insurance. Above all, he says, "The farmer must have a sympathetic and understanding Administration which believes in farmers and will fight for farmers' interests."

When a farmer fights for parity, Symington says, he is not fighting for excess profits. His fight is for equality, because 100 per cent parity actually represents nothing more than equality. But the farmer does not even ask for 100 per cent parity. He asks for 90 per cent parity on some crops, less on others.

As to the huge surplus, Symington has two plans:

Use it to promote world friendship; and stockpile part of it for possible emergencies.

"We can and should use the productive genius of American farmers to promote our goals in the world," he asserts. "Food can be used to strengthen our ties with the underdeveloped countries. Why not strengthen those ties with food, of which we have plenty, instead of dollars, with which we are having increasing troubles?

"It is a sin to waste food when people are hungry. It is worse than a sin when this food could have been used to help build a peaceful world."

Some months ago Symington introduced a bill in the Senate to stockpile food, medical supplies, and other basic items necessary for survival in case this country is ever attacked with modern weapons. Other bills introduced by him were for distribution of food and clothing to needy families, for expanding the school-lunch program, for establishing a food-fiber stamp plan to help get surplus food and clothing to the needy, and for giving some of it to public health, educational and research institutions and programs.

"What a paradox!" he exclaims. "A farm program designed to reduce production ends up in increasing production. It is true that our present surpluses are high, and that they have increased tremendously during the last seven years. As long as millions of the world's population go to bed hungry every night, and while we are continuing to send billions of dollars in foreign aid, why not substitute more bushels for dollars?

"In the cities and towns of our own America we have between 15 and 20 million people who are undernourished. A recent food consumption study found that 10 per cent of all families interviewed had a diet below minimum standards. With such conditions in our country, surely we can achieve better use of our farm surpluses."

On a sore point with every housewife who goes to market for her family's groceries, he brings out an indisputable fact:

"The Department of Agriculture has been conducting a continuous campaign to lead the American people to believe that the present reduction in farm income would reduce the retail price of food.

"But has it done so? Far from it. Food prices have not gone down—they have gone up, and up. And at the same time the farmer's share of the consumer food dollar has gone down. Somewhere in that spread between producer and consumer something is unhealthy and wrong. It is something that must and will be studied."

Of particular concern to Symington is the peril today of the very existence of the one-family farm in America.

"It's inconceivable to me that the family-size farm should cease to be a pleasant part of America," he says. "If the family-size farm disappears, with it will disappear the small town, and if our country is characterized by giantism on the farm and giantism in industry, a few great cities, a few great factory farms, it would not be the America, or the way of life we know and love.

"Since World War II this country has spent hundreds of millions of dollars encouraging the preservation of family-size farms in other countries. But here at home we have not really spent a cent for that purpose. In fact the reverse is true—the policies of Benson's Department of Agriculture have been encouraging farm mergers.

"It's sad but true that in recent years half a million farm families—that is, millions of farm people—have left the land; and that is a trend that must be stopped."

4

In the theory and practice of efficiency and good management in either business or Government, Stuart Symington speaks with authority that none can very successfully dispute. His record of bringing order out of chaos, and smooth-working power to business after business, and Government department after department, is too impressive to deny. So when he discusses Government organization, or lack of it, he has something to say that comes from practical knowledge.

"America," he says, "hasn't even scratched the surface of its vast potential, and the world and the space around it can be our heritage, if we get better planning, better men, better coordination."

Today, he says, the Government is bogged down in bureaucratic waste, far worse than ever in the much-maligned Truman Administration, worse than in any Administration in history.

"Better management can uncover $5 billion to $10 billion a year in present Federal resources which now is being thrown away," he says.

The difficulty is inducing able men to devote their time and talents to the business of the Nation. In a measure he feels this is due to apathy or a wrong attitude toward Government.

"There are dedicated public servants in this country, men who are willing to sacrifice personal gain for the labor of helping run the Government. But too often you won't find men who will make that necessary sacrifice. Making money is more important to them than the good of their country."

Symington remembers that when he took over the administration of one of the Government departments he offered a key job—an important one—to thirty-four men before he found one who would take it. All the others rather scorned him for staying in Government, when he could be "out making money" in the postwar era.

"They criticize," he says, "but they won't step in and give their time and ability."

As to the type of businessman needed, he has well-formed opinions. "Big business" is not the touchstone. He considers that the "super-efficiency" of big business is a myth, and this from personal observation. He competed against big business, and sold to big business. He was the "little company" fighting the giants.

"They used to say to me, 'How big do you want to get Emerson?'" he reminisces. "I'd say, 'Never so big that we're not being persecuted by General Electric and Westinghouse.' I was always proud of being a small businessman."

He knows the bureaucracies in giant corporations and how they, too, waste money; and he feels that the good little operator is more efficient, gives the consumers a better buy.

"The trouble is that this Administration looks for 'big name executives'—who are ready to retire," he says. "But this worship of people who get into the big name jobs isn't always borne out, by any means, in the men themselves.

"You take a lot of those fellows. They hitch their wagon to a—sometimes it turns out to be a star—sometimes it turns out to be a lemon. If its' a star they get big. If it's a lemon they are nothing. But the point is, they hitch on, instead of pulling.

"But you give me the man that made his own way. I like the fellow who's been through the mill in competitive business, building up his own little company. Maybe he's overextended himself and lost everything. That man learned something in the experience.

"Take the man who starts out, gets a payroll to meet, perhaps gets licked. He comes back, tries some more, gets a drug store maybe, buys some more, fails in a couple, gets two then six, and then the first thing you know, he's got six hundred.

"That's the kind of man for me, when it comes to problems that are original and new. Anybody can follow the chart of bureaucracy, whether in business or government.

"The trouble is that often, in one of those great corporations, when a fellow bothers them they say, 'Well, let's give him to the Government—he's getting senile.' That's probably not quite the way they put it, but that's what's in the backs of their minds.

"So they come down here to Washington, and they say, 'We'll make a *great* sacrifice. We're going to let you have one of our biggest men.' Then they turn the old boy over to the Government, and there he is. And his wife comes down here, and he gets a car, and a chauffeur, and sometimes a flag. He's quite a boy—and you've got just what you don't want. What hurts the Government and the country and all America in a case like that, is that there are thousands of people who would do a much better job than he ever will, or could."

Symington's labors for efficiency date back to his earliest days in the executive field of Government. Though he knows fully that politics differs from business, he is sure that enormous improvements in getting better work and saving taxpayers' money can be made by vigorous study and action in the Executive branch of Government.

"There have been some surprisingly unbusinesslike operations on the part of this so-called Business Administration," he says. "Government waste, inefficiency and corruption can be as dangerous to our people as aggression from without."

XIX

"ONE ISSUE?"
OR "BIGGEST ISSUE?"

1

Relatively recently some politicians who have begun to see Stuart Symington as a serious factor to be dealt with in the political chess game that is coming with the advancing months of 1960, have studied his record with an eye to finding flaws in it.

Perhaps somewhat to their consternation, they found very few things that could even by broadest interpretation be labeled as "weaknesses." His position on such matters as education, agriculture, economics, foreign policy, foreign trade and tariff, labor, social security, civil rights, and national defense are open, clear—and sound.

So lacking any more cogent argument against him, a trial balloon was sent up in the form of a magazine article, published in July 1959, which Holmes Alexander described as "speaking through its author for some Democratic leaders who obviously don't want Symington to win the [Presidential] nomination, and who are afraid he might."

That article, plainly biased, and just as plainly untrue, described Senator Symington as a man with only "one issue," who has made little vocal appearance in the Senate, is staff led, and is reluctant to take a stand on any matter.

It is perhaps true that Symington's long battle for adequate national defense has strongly identified him with that issue in the public mind. But to say that national defense is his sole issue is about as silly as to say, for example, that the Government itself, because national defense is its biggest concern, on which the greatest slice of its budget is expended, has national defense as its only function.

He is one of the Senate's top agricultural experts, and has fought hard for the farmer. He is deeply interested in Government efficiency, not only in the Pentagon but in all administrative departments. In foreign policy matters he has taken a vital part, and it was he who introduced the Economic Disarmament Resolution.

On the controversial matters which some Senators tiptoe quietly about, such as civil rights and labor, both his public statements and his history of past actions show a position both courageous and constructive, which all can understand.

Symington is not, to be sure, one of your bell-tongued Senators. He is a man of action rather than of words, and when he speaks he is inclined to be brief and to the point. By instinct and training he is a well-disciplined "get things done" type of individual, and he sometimes grows a little restive under time-wasting oratory, when it accomplishes nothing except to get the speaker additional pages in the *Congressional Record*.

As a matter of fact, though he devotes himself to the hard work of committee hearings and deliberations where the real labors of the Senate are performed, he speaks frequently enough, though rarely at great length. The record of his speeches on the floor of the Senate in 1958 shows that he made exactly the same number (twenty-six each) on defense and agriculture, only a few less on national economics, with a number on foreign affairs and disarmament, several on the labor situation, and the rest on assorted subjects.

Can it be possible, some quarters are beginning to ask themselves, that there is a method in his policy of hard work and a comparative absence of the hortatory and the diffuse in the speeches he does make?

Has Symington reasoned out the fact that one of the big reasons why Senators so rarely have become Presidents in the past is that they talk *too* much? And has he tried to avoid that mistake—and shrewdly succeeded?

At least it is now becoming evident that he has quietly gone about his business, built a fine record, and made no unnecessary enemies. And also that the "one issue" innuendo should be edited to read "biggest issue" perhaps, but by no means the only one in which this widely integrated man is interested and for which he is working.

One little matter overlooked by not a few on the political scene, at least until comparatively recently, is the fact that over the years Symington has become a pretty fair politician himself, and in the best sense of the word. He has the highest respect for politics and believes it is the only way a democracy can work.

"Politics has been defined as the science of the operation of Government," he says. "But I've known a few great statesmen who disagreed even with that definition. They contend that politics in reality is an art, the art of persuading people in the right direction; and surely that adds pleasure to anyone's approach to Government, whether as an interest, or as a career."

All this has caused potential rivals to regard him with heightened respect.

It is just possible that Stuart Symington can take his place at the political chessboard and hold his own with other masters of the art of gambit and checkmate.

2

When the Declaration of Independence was written, in committee, but largely by Thomas Jefferson, the emphasis was on the *responsibilities* of citizenship. By the time the Constitution was drawn up eleven years later, the emphasis had shifted to *rights*.

Both are good, but the difference is that responsibilities are toward others, while rights are toward self. To maintain the latter, there must be men who will accept the former, even at personal sacrifice. The men who have been willing to shoulder responsibilities stand out like lofty towers in our national history.

In this matter of responsibility, Stuart Symington has a singularly vivid history of accepting heavy burdens willingly, and brilliantly carrying them forward to successful conclusions. His six trouble-shooting executive jobs each was a matter of taking on responsibility under difficult conditions, and each ended in a splendid accomplishment. His going to the Senate instead of to an easier and perhaps more pleasant life with much money and lush living, was due to a sheer feeling of responsibility to his country and its people, in a situation of danger which he recognized perhaps more clearly than almost anyone else.

In the Senate he has not hesitated to shoulder responsibility, when it was necessary.

His very duel with McCarthy was criticized by some of the more "realistic" Democrats on the ground that McCarthy was a Republican problem, and the Democrats had only to sit back while he destroyed the Republican President. But Symington saw the McCarthy threat as one affecting the very core of national defense, and did his duty as a citizen and an American.

On his own responsibility he withheld publication of the findings of the Air Force inquiry, though some members of his party wanted it for campaign ammunition. It was too important, he felt, for political considerations, and released it only after the election was over and the new Congress in session.

But he is a good party man, with a thorough belief in the philosophy and purposes of the Democratic Party.

"The Democratic Party has more than vitality," he says. "It has wisdom—and it has patriotism. We Democrats understand thoroughly that the country's good comes always before the welfare of the party. The Democratic Party believes that what is best for America is also best for the Democratic Party —and not the other way around."

His general attitude toward the usefulness of the political parties is wholesome and well thought out. He expressed it in these words in a speech at Kansas City:

"I am not much concerned that politics is the comedian's target. In fact, we'd be in pretty sad shape if politics and politicians were immune from kidding.

"What does concern me is the serious, usually misinformed, type of criticism which condemns partisan politics as cheap or unworthy. . . .

"I believe with Disraeli that 'party is organized opinion.' Parties give the voters a choice of opposing policies. Parties are the antagonists in the great debate which we call democracy. And where there are no parties, there is no democracy."

In the last election he illustrated his party loyalty rather interestingly.

A cousin of his, Fife Symington, was running for Congress on the Republican ticket in a Maryland district. Opposed to him was Dan Brewster, a Democrat.

The Symington name means much in Maryland, and the Republican candidate quite naturally capitalized on it. His billboards read: SYMINGTON FOR CONGRESS. And they did not specify clearly which Symington it was.

Fearing the voters might be misled, Brewster appealed to the Senator. Stuart Symington's solution was characteristically direct. He had himself photographed with Brewster, his arm around the candidate's shoulder, and wrote a letter:

> Dear Dan: Like yourself I am a lifelong Democrat and believe it vitally important for the future of our Nation that we elect a Democratic Congress. Therefore, if I lived in your district, I would vote the straight Democratic ticket, and of course that means I would vote for you. Sincerely yours, Stuart Symington.

Dan Brewster was delighted. He used the picture and letter in his campaign, and was elected.

3

Although he deprecates his own speaking ability, and prefers to rely on facts rather than rhetoric, Symington is in reality a very effective speaker, particularly when his blood is up. He is slow to ire, genuinely likes a pleasant atmosphere, dislikes offending anyone. But when an issue arises on which he has strong convictions he can be a very tough fighter.

"He likes to say yes," says his friend, Congressman Brown of Missouri. "But he is cautious until he gets a complete grasp, and then all hell can't budge him. A 'no' is a 'no.' He has a deep inner core of hard steel. He knows where this country ought to go, and what he wants to do about it, and he will at times give and take on 'fringe' stuff. But on the basics he will not yield an inch."

Symington names six men as having most influenced his life, and his viewpoints.

"Of course, there was my father," he says. "He was the rare combination of an athlete and a thinker. At Johns Hopkins he was Phi Beta Kappa, took his Ph.D. in French folklore, and was captain of the football team. He was also on the Druids, a lacrosse team in Baltimore which won the national championship. He gave me respect for knowledge and a lifetime habit of research and many other things.

"One of his brothers, Donald Symington, was a top industrialist. He had a passion for facts, which he transmitted to me. He was a poor banker because he loaned too much money to his friends in the depression; but he did a lot to train me in industrial management philosophies.

"The next person, perhaps, who made a deep impression on me was an Irishman, Dave O'Brien, former vice president of Graybar Electric. He was cynical, brilliant, liberal—an Irishman out of County Cork, who began as a telephone lineman in New York and became one of the ablest businessmen I have ever known.

"Governor O. Max Gardner of North Carolina, whose wife once told me he considered me as a son, was my lawyer and friend until his death on his way to England to be our Ambassador. He had been Governor of his state, was senior partner of his law firm in Washington, and was a wise, kind and thoughtful friend with some high ideals of politics.

"Another very close friend is Bishop Will Scarlett, who probably did as much as anybody in forming my thinking. He was the Episcopal Bishop of Missouri, and before that of Arizona, a former cowpuncher and Harvard graduate. Now retired, but beloved because of his sympathies for all people, 'Bishop Will' was often used as a referee in labor disputes. He is a great Christian, truly spiritual, and yet with wonderful practical common sense.

"Then of course there was my father-in-law, Senator James Wadsworth, a very great man. He was completely devoted to his country, and had profound belief in the democratic principles of Government. He was a hard-headed politician, but never stooped to anything unethical, and his genuine patriotism made a lasting impression on me. He and Governor Gardner probably were the most influential in giving me respect for Government and a sense of responsibility to the people of the Nation."

Among Symington's near associates in Washington and elsewhere today there is a wide variety in personalities. Among them are these:

Clark Clifford, a brilliant lawyer originally from St. Louis, served in the Navy as a Commander during World War II, was assigned from active service in the Pacific front to the White House on special duty, and stayed on as legal advisor to President Harry S. Truman. He now leads his own law firm in Washington, and is a close friend and legal advisor to Symington.

A man with an attractive personality and a fine legal mind, some say Clark Clifford is Symington's Number One advisor. It is certain that he has tremendous influence with the Senator, and also that he is genuinely fond of Symington and devoted to him.

Another lawyer, James Meredith of St. Louis, has been campaign manager for Stuart Symington in two Senatorial elections. He is a practical politician, with intimate knowledge of the countless details which are necessary in gearing a campaign into smooth-running action, and he and the Senator are friends of long standing who have been through many battles side by side.

Meredith set up a legal practice in St. Louis after the first Symington campaign of 1952 and has been very successful in it. In the firm with him is Tim (Stuart, Jr.) Symington.

One of the Senator's closest confidants and friends is Congressman Charley Brown, of the southwest Missouri district which includes the cities of Springfield and Joplin. Brown is comparatively new to politics, being at this writing in his second term in Congress, but that he is a better than fair hand at it is proved by his extraordinary record. A radio and television executive, he had as a young man made speeches for Democratic candidates, but never entered the game himself until the election of 1956.

At that time the perennial incumbent was the veteran Dewey Short, Republican, who had held the seat since 1929. As a matter of fact the Republicans had sent a Congressman from that district almost without a break since the Civil War.

Brown, who is a slow-speaking, humorous, companionable man, conceals underneath this easy-going exterior one of the keenest brains in Congress. When he decided to run against Short nobody thought he had a chance, but he introduced some new ideas into his campaigning, and in the year of the Eisenhower landslide, he unseated his opponent for the first time, running up a majority of a bare 1,000 votes. In the next election he won by 10,000.

In its way, though on a somewhat smaller scale, his victories were as much of an upset as were Symington's in the Senate races.

Symington enjoys Brown's company, and listens to him. Brown shares the Senator's high ideals of public service, and the two of them often consult on issues, putting their heads together on knotty problems, political or otherwise.

Among Symington's close friends in the Senate is Hubert Humphrey of Minnesota. The Missouri Senator has deep respect for Humphrey's mind and integrity, and the sentiment is returned by the Minnesota Senator.

Sam Rayburn, Speaker of the House, served in Congress with Senator Wadsworth, Eve Symington's father. Though Mr. Rayburn is a Democrat and Wadsworth was a Republican the two were close personal friends. "Mr. Sam" is quite fond of both Eve and Stuart Symington. The distinguished Texan is a sort of father confessor, politically speaking, to most of the younger generation of Democrats in Congress, and this is true of Symington. It is possible that the Senator would take the counsel of Mr. Sam over any other political advice.

Two members of Symington's staff are especially close and valuable to him. They are Stanley R. Fike, administrative assistant, and Dr. Edward C. Welsh, expert on economics and defense matters as well as many other things.

Fike is referred to by the Senator as his "right arm," and upon him Symington depends tremendously. Easy-going and pleasant in manner, he gives you the impression of thinking every minute; and this indeed is necessary in his case, for he is in charge of multitudinous details which he handles

smoothly and, as far as is humanly possible, without confusion.

He is clear-headed and calm, does not stampede, and is
always on the watch for "jokers" someone might try to slip
into a political deck of cards. He clears information, screens
visitors, and sees to it that the interests of his state are taken
care of. Stanley Fike, indeed, is frequently called "Missouri's
third Senator" because of his services to that commonwealth.
So loyal is he to Symington that he turned down an almost
certain chance to replace a recently deceased Congressman
from Independence, Missouri, to stay with the Senator. A
former newspaper man, Fike also is in charge of press releases
and his acquaintance in the journalistic fraternity is very wide.

Dr. Edward C. Welsh is brilliant and learned, a remarkable
research man and a veritable walking library of information.

"I like to get things clear," says Senator Symington. "I've
always been envious and respectful of my beloved friend,
Bernard M. Baruch, who is very proud of the fact that they
call him 'Mr. Facts.'"

When information is wanted, Dr. Welsh is the "Mr.
Facts" of the Symington staff. Keen and precise in his thinking, he knows where to go to get what is wanted, if he does
not happen to have it already in his apparently almost in-
exhaustible store of data stored in his head.

He has held numerous important posts, and after a tour
of duty in occupied Japan during which he was a member of
the Foreign Investment Board of Japan, he was specially
honored by the Army for his major contributions to the development of private enterprise in that country. He has been
with Symington since the old NSRB days, was a member of
numerous commissions to foreign countries in the RFC
period, and is a key figure in the present organization.

Symington is proud of his entire staff, but there is no question about its being his staff and he the boss. Information he asks for is always to buttress or otherwise bear on his own original thinking. Countless details are handled in his office, but he lays down the rules, and when a decision is to be made, the decision is his alone. The staff and its functioning are exactly what you might expect to find under a superior manager like Stuart Symington.

XX

STUART SYMINGTON TODAY

1

The Stuart Symington of today is an older, wiser, more experienced, but not less energetic and imaginative, edition of the Stuart Symington who met his first great challenge at Emerson Electric in 1938. His hair is graying, but his finely conditioned, athletic body, and his expressive face give you an impression of vigor which is well borne out by his activities on any typical day.

That day always begins early for him, whether the Senate is in session or not. Customarily, he arises at six to six-thirty o'clock in the morning. He is a close and careful newspaper reader, and by the time he arrives at his office, he has the news columns thoroughly digested, and much other work accomplished.

The office opens for work at eight-thirty o'clock in the morning. When it closes depends on the work that must be done, and sometimes members of the staff labor long after six o'clock, along with the "Boss."

As an example, on a recent national holiday, a friend on the Pacific Coast wished to get in touch with him on some matter, and because it was a national holiday, telephoned by long distance to Symington's house in Georgetown. There was no answer. The friend remembered that the Senator allows himself the pleasure and exercise of a game of golf when he has time for it, so he called the club where he usually plays. No Symington.

Next the friend tried to get the Senator's secretary, Mrs. Virginia Laird, at her home, thinking she might know where the Senator would be on that day. She was gone. He tried Stanley Fike and Dr. Welsh in succession. A blank each time.

Suddenly a great light broke over the West Coast friend. He had the operator dial Symington's *office*—and there they were, all of them including the Senator, and the place was humming with activity. Something needed to be done, and they were doing it.

When Symington is on the Senate floor the staff has its hands full enough, but when he arrives in his private office at the rear of the suite of rooms assigned to him—and he usually lets himself in by a door at the back—things really begin to jump. His buzzer summons members of his staff in rapid succession, sometimes two or three at a time, for requests or directions.

He has a remarkable ability to keep in mind several matters at once, and often gives instructions to an aide or two while carrying on a telephone conversation—and never with any confusion among the various subjects on which his wonderfully elastic mind takes hold, one after another, or even interchangeably.

Mrs. Virginia Laird, whose husband is an Air Force Colonel, has been his secretary ever since he was Assistant Secretary of War for Air, back in 1946—longer than anyone else on his staff. An extremely competent and intelligent person, she has this estimate of her "Boss":

He is kindly and considerate to his staff members, preferring to ask rather than command, and is quick to praise good work. But he insists on efficiency and if something goes wrong, especially if it is due to any kind of neglect or lack of promptness, he can be impatient, even sharp.

He works long hours, longer than any of his staff, sometimes at great tension; and his staff is completely loyal to him, and finds it a pleasure to work overtime if necessary, because he carries it along with him by his enthusiasm and the importance of his purpose.

He has an incredibly retentive memory, and when he is getting a report on something he has an almost uncanny ability to put his finger on the salient points in a long array of information—"like an electric scanner, almost."

When he is preparing a speech, he will talk it over with members of his staff, and listen carefully to their opinions on the subject. Perhaps one or two of them may write a draft for him. But in the end he writes his own speeches. He will consider the drafts, and then he will sit back in his chair, maybe look off into space, and dictate the entire speech himself.

"What a lot of people don't realize is that he is a superb phrase maker."

When he talks, he knows what he is talking about, or he won't talk. And he is extremely patient and careful with his explanations if anyone has difficulty following him, until he is sure that everything is straight.

He does not care for a "phony"—and he can spot them almost as soon as they walk into the room.

Finally, he is the most dedicated man Mrs. Laird ever knew, and the word "patriotism" is no cliché with him. He lives it.

Not every man earns a tribute like that from his secretary.

2

On the Senate floor Symington is distinguished and handsome in appearance. Not only is he a statesman, but he *looks* the part, and the two are not often found in such notable combination.

His recipe for statesmanship—although he never uses that word with reference to himself—is hard work, hard thinking, the ability to understand motives of men and nations, and a clear realization of the greatest good for one's own country.

Among his colleagues he is popular, and there is usually a group of men around him with friendly smiles on their faces. He can be relaxed and charming, tell a humorous story intimately—and in the next instant become all intense concentration when some serious matter arises in the discussion.

His heavy labors in committee and in the full Senate sessions, which have been described, do not cease when he is away from Capitol Hill. He often takes his work home with him, if it is something that has to be thought out or done at once.

When he first entered Government work, back in the early period of the Surplus Property Board, Symington had a reputation of being hard for reporters to interview. He was at that time, it must be remembered, a fairly young businessman, freshly drafted to do the job, without knowledge of politics, and with a businessman's somewhat typical uneasiness, the fear that he might be misquoted or wrongly represented by what the business world then regarded—and still does—as a strange and mysterious and somehow perilous breed—the newspaper fraternity.

The years have changed that. His recognition of the press

as the great medium for getting information to the people was shown by his anxiety to get a superior public relations man when he took charge of the RFC.

No longer is he uneasy with reporters, and though he is still sensitive and considered somewhat thin-skinned, he has learned to laugh off most criticism, even when they are unjust.

In point of fact he has a genuine liking for the type of people who write for newspapers or magazines, or are commentators on radio or television, because he considers them especially alert, well informed, and eager to get the facts, which are qualities he admires.

In this connection, Symington charges that the Administration conceals pertinent facts from the people, which they have a right to know, and should know. Security matters, he holds, must be protected, but other public affairs should be open and candid.

"The strength of the Nation depends on the will of the people," is the way he states it. "But in a democratic form of government, that will can only function if the people are informed."

Also, "Partial truth is an evasion of truth. Let the people have the truth; they will do whatever is necessary to remain free."

With newsmen he tries to be approachable and helpful. In an interview he is inclined to talk rapidly, because he thinks rapidly, but he is always willing to halt and explain or elaborate on a statement, or answer a question. If, for some good reason, he cannot answer, he will not beat about the bush. He will simply say, "I'm afraid I can't discuss that." And if it is possible to give the reason why—as, for example, that it is privileged information—he will do so.

Occasionally he may express himself rather forcefully on something. At such times he is apt to pause, grin, and say. "You'll have to be careful with that," and trust to the discretion and honesty of his interviewer.

His memory is phenomenal and his analyses keen. In general he talks in the vernacular, with easy use of sports phrases or slang expressions, unless he is making some sort of a formal utterance. His ordinary speech is as freely and typically American as he himself is.

He has a habit of saying, "See what I mean?" and looking inquiringly at the person to whom he is speaking, to make sure his meaning is clear. Few fail to see what he means when he finishes an explanation.

Summing up his whole attitude toward the press, he says: "The real truth will never get you into trouble."

3

When Congress is in session, Senator and Mrs. Symington live in an old eighteenth-century brick house in Georgetown, a suburb of Washington. It was formerly the home of Senator and Mrs. Wadsworth, and still belongs to Eve Symington's mother.

Georgetown was a prosperous city, with cobblestone streets and fashionable inns long before Washington itself was built, and the present Symington residence was erected in 1790, the very year that the neighboring "swampy waste" was selected by George Washington as the site for what he called the Federal City, and before L'Enfant had even laid out the plan for the capital in its present form.

The cobblestones have been replaced with more modern paving, but otherwise the house looks much as it did in those old days, and it is filled with tradition. It is built in the eighteenth century style when each house had a common wall with its neighbors on either side, thus forming a solid row of dwellings down the street. A wrought-iron railing on the steps leading up to the front door would catch any collector's eye.

Within, the home is pleasant, informal, and hospitable. It is distinctive for some very valuable oil paintings by old masters, historic antiques, and mementos of many kinds, gathered chiefly by Eve Symington's famous grandfather, John Hay, or her equally famous father, Senator Wadsworth.

The Symingtons have comparatively little time to themselves, but they have a power of deeply enjoying what they have. The Senator does not smoke, and only occasionally takes a cocktail—*one*—to be sociable in an evening. But he and Mrs. Symington are so delightful as companions that they are in very great demand for dinners and parties both formal and informal in the Nation's capital.

Eve Symington is the sort of woman who was born to shine in any surroundings, attractive, warmly friendly, gay, even brilliant in her conversation. She does not go in for club work or make speeches, but her charm and sincerity have won for her a very large circle of devoted friends.

As for the Senator, during an evening with good company, he delights in lying back in a comfortable chair, with one long leg dangling over the arm, or perhaps both feet propped up, and range the fields of discourse. Invariably he is interested in what others say, and he has a quick and ready appreciation of either the sage or the witty in conversation.

Until recently, talk about Presidential possibilities has been more or less tabooed, but he laughed quite heartily when someone showed him the following statement by witty Congressman Celler of New York, offering his appraisal of the Democratic White House possibilities for 1960:

"There's Senator Douglas, he's too old; Senator Kennedy, he's too young; Governor Meyner, he's too minor; Senator Humphrey, he's too talkative; Senator Johnson, he's too South; Governor Williams, he's too soapy; Adlai Stevenson, he's too often; Senator Symington, he's my man!"

Yet his actions are not those of a man made jittery by being bitten by a Presidential bug. Rather they are those of a Senator doing his duty, instead of nervously hunting candidates for a convention battle.

Sometimes he expresses, in more serious vein, theories that are always interesting:

"A successful man in business, or in running an executive department, must try to move forward into decisions with clarity and get things settled. All my life, I've tried to reduce matters to where even *I* could understand them. I find that people who have the name of being 'intellectuals' seldom quite get down to what is definite.

"Now, when you have to say to a person—especially around politics where things can get vague anyway—when you have to say to such a person, 'I beg your pardon, I don't understand what you're trying to say. What is it you mean?' And when you say that two or three times, they think you're rude.

"I remember when I was Secretary of the Air Force, the Secretary of Defense rather fell for a certain fellow, who was supposed to be an expert on Russia. The first time I heard this man talk, I thought he was great. The second time, I thought I was nuts. The sixth time, I thought *he* was nuts. So we quit even."

With that came the Symington chuckle.

Or, thinking out loud, he says:

"Of course the real test of a man in public life today is: What share of America should the people have? Do you believe in purchasing power at the base? Do you believe in raw capitalism, unbridled, unrestricted? Must it be the very few who are rich and millions who are very poor?

"I believe in purchasing power at the base. And I know that management and labor can work together compatibly. I've settled strikes that were destroying good companies. I've handled union leaders that management said were 'impossible.' Workers have their rights and their legitimate requests.

"Too many businessmen are afraid of the workers, have a chip on their shoulders, don't even try to reach agreements. These businessmen bring their attitude into Government when they come here.

"They have deep prejudices, shared by their fellow members of the Union League Club. They talk only to their prejudiced friends, refuse to think, just feel that anyone who is a successful businessman wears a 'white hat' [is a hero], and the ordinary people wear 'black hats' [are on the wrong side]. Fear prompts them to resist every new idea, every social or economic reform, because it might bolster the position of the ordinary people who—they feel—are trying to gain at the expense of the businessman. They can't seem to get the concept that the businessman gains when the ordinary people gain."

All of this is without rancor. Symington is a businessman himself, and on the subject of resistance to new ideas and reforms on the part of a certain segment of the more reactionary businessmen he is concerned, but far from resentful, because he sees both sides.

On the whole subject of business and labor relations, he speaks with singular authority.

He is the only one of the men most prominently mentioned in the Presidential talk today who has ever made a conspicuous success outside of politics, and he was a brilliant industrialist, who knows what it is to build up a company from nothing to where it is worth millions to its stockholders, and do it over and over.

He has worked for a living with his hands, and he labored in sweat and dirt and heat for years, while he studied at night to improve himself.

He is the only one who knows both sides of the question: what it is to be on the payroll, what it is to meet the payroll.

He alone can talk with businessmen in their own terms, with laboring men in theirs.

In politics, he is the only one who has displayed outstanding ability in both the executive and legislative branches of Government.

Of them all he has most brilliantly shown that he has what psychologists call "the great power of adaptation," which fits him supremely to cope with problems of every nature, under every condition.

4

Stuart Symington, fifty-eight years old and in his prime physically and mentally, is today one of the salient figures in America.

As to the Presidency, he shows his interest in what is going on, and his pleasure over the growing talk of his candidacy, but he has remained aloof from the state primary contests, although he has accepted an unprecedented—for him—number of out-state speaking engagements in recent months. His manner even in these platform appearances is easy, friendly, and relaxed, rather than showing any traces of the tense, hard-driving candidate, as usually seen.

The *Press-Herald* of Portland, Maine, recently said of him editorially:

> In the paradoxical game of politics, the race doesn't always go to the candidate who runs fastest; it sometimes goes to the man who sits by the side of the road, contemplatively chewing a blade of grass and watching the others go by.
>
> As of the moment the Democratic Party's roadside sitter is Missouri's tall, soft-spoken Senator Stuart Symington.
>
> . . . Symington isn't going to knock himself out trying to catch up with the hard-running front runners for the Presidential nomination . . .
>
> Symington sits, smiles—and gains ground.
>
> This is not to say he is completely motionless, or apathetic, or uninterested. It is simply that his tactics are different from those of the . . . school of maximum exertion.
>
> Symington for the nonce is content with his seat by the side of the road. Judging from recent opinion polls, and the general reaction here in Maine, it is a profitable position for him to be in.

That *may* be a shrewd analysis.

One thing is dead certain.

Stuart Symington believes with all his heart that men as well as nations must accept responsibility, and follow policies that create events, rather than waiting for events to create their policies.

If he were asked by his party and his Nation to face the final, greatest challenge that all history has offered a single man, in this nuclear-space age of vast changing tides and crises, there is no doubt whatsoever what his answer would be.